The
Escape to the Country
Handbook

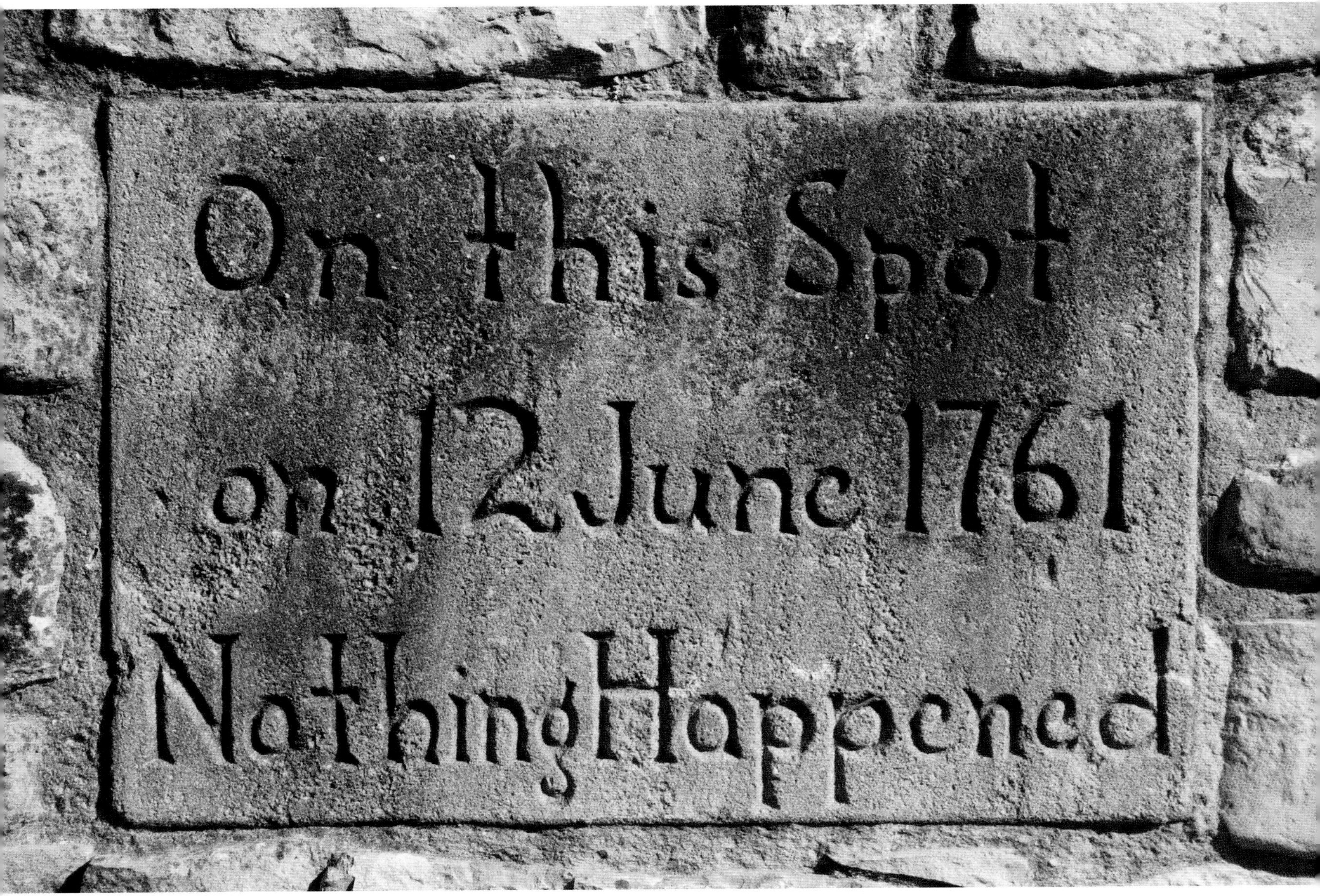
On this Spot
on 12 June 1761
Nothing Happened

The
Escape to the Country
Handbook

Jules Hudson

First published in the United Kingdom in 2020 by
National Trust Books
43 Great Ormond Street
London
WC1N 3HZ

An imprint of Pavilion Books Group Ltd

ISBN: 9781911358909

A CIP catalogue record for this book is available from the British Library.

10 9 8 7 6 5 4 3 2 1

Reproduction by Rival Colour Ltd, UK
Printed and bound by Toppan Leefung Printing Ltd, China

This book is available at National Trust shops and online at www.nationaltrustbooks.co.uk, or try the publisher (www.pavilionbooks.com) or your local bookshop.

Contents

For Mum and Dad, Tania and Jack, with much love, J x

INTRODUCTION

My first Escape to the Country in the Cambrian Mountains of Mid Wales.

For most of my adult life, I've had the good fortune to live and work in the countryside. I grew up in Colchester, in the heart of Britain's oldest recorded town, which can uniquely trace its roots back to the fascinating threshold between the Iron Age and the arrival of the Romans who set about creating their first capital there. Yet, as a keen young horseman, from the age of 11, I spent every free moment out in the local countryside with Honey, a beautiful dun-coloured Connemara mare. Together we explored miles of woodlands and tracks as we grew up side by side through my teens and into my early twenties. Embracing the independence of riding together or in company we made the countryside our own and it inspired a visceral appreciation of the great outdoors. Born a townie, this early discovery of an innate connection to wild natural spaces and what it took to live there has long convinced me that as human beings we are all country folk at heart.

Eventually I embarked upon a career as an archaeologist, a life-changing ambition that took me to the small Welsh market town of Lampeter in West Wales, and to its even smaller university. I moved into a tiny holiday let in an ancient farming village in the heart of the Cambrian Mountains and began an intense love affair with the rugged open uplands that surrounded me. This stunning rural location inspired me to learn, through the prism of the past, how our material human history had developed, and how we had marked a landscape that I was in effect learning to read. Understanding and recognising this human shaping of the natural world and the evolving pattern of settlement and architecture has since been a fascinating handrail in making sense of the world around me.

This early stage in my life had a profound effect. Not only did I come to relish the contextual understanding of the British landscape, I also set about finding a home of my own in the hills. Aged just 26 I found my first Escape to the Country; a small stone cottage in the village that had first welcomed me to Wales, Llanddewi Brefi. Some 200 years old and derelict, it was this small neglected building that instilled in me a love of renovation and of rural life that enveloped me like a long-lost family, and it remained my home for the best part of 20 years.

An early career as a field archaeologist eventually led me to a life in television, first in production and then crossing the tracks to become a presenter. Out of the blue, a surprise invitation to host *Escape to the Country* for the BBC over a decade ago proved to be a turning point for which I shall be forever grateful. At a stroke, it provided the opportunity to share my passion for country life and to help others transform their own aspirations for a country life into reality.

Since then I have met many couples along the way. Every encounter is unique, yet each couple shares the same aim. I remain forever indebted to the hundreds of people with whom I've had the privilege of sharing what is a very personal endeavour, to seek out their ideal home, often transforming their lives in the same profound way that finding my home did for mine.

Eventually I felt the lessons of this ongoing voyage of discovery might be worth drawing together in a book. It gives me great pleasure to share what I have learnt. I have made these discoveries in the most inspiring and learned of company, be they buyers, our wonderful production teams, or the countless experts I have worked with along the way, both professionally and at home. If you too are thinking that country life might be for you, give it a go. Life comes but once, and in my experience the countryside, and country folk, will help you make exactly what you want of it.

Happy house hunting!

How to use this book

For many of us, making a life-changing move to a new destination can be daunting, and no more so than for those wishing to Escape to the Country.

Knowing where to look is a key consideration when planning your great escape. The UK has a huge amount to offer, but that's easy to say if you have done as much research as we have on the series. For most buyers, the chance to spend a lifetime exploring the British Isles is not an option.

One of the key aims of this handbook is to highlight, in broad terms, what some of the most popular regions of the country can offer as regards their cultural identity, architectural styles and budgetary implications. For well over a decade on *Escape to the Country* we have advised thousands of buyers while at the same time building up in-depth knowledge of the very diverse and appealing rural hotspots that Britain's countryside provides.

Part I of the book focuses on the practical aspects of planning a move. It is essential to be as informed as possible when making this kind of decision and this section includes information on everything you will need to consider, from where to go, the type of property to buy and the things to bear in mind when you are making your final choice.

One of the great appeals of moving to a country property is the chance to live in a home endowed with more history and character than many of us have lived in before. Historic country properties are without doubt the most popular aspect of what the series has championed, from rambling and cosy cottages to sprawling farmhouses and manors. Famously, our pick of the much favoured 'mystery house' has allowed us to showcase some of the nation's most memorable homes, from converted chapels, windmills and

castles (at least one of which even came with the title of lord/lady of the manor), to modern grand designs. But of course, older properties do come with some strings, from the level of maintenance they require through to the fact that many are listed, a factor which can put some buyers off, in my view needlessly. We have included chapters on 'Taking on a project', 'Listed buildings' and 'Living with thatch', plus a brief guide to what to do when planning your annual maintenance schedule.

The chapter on 'Running your country home' offers advice on essential services, with a section on fires and wood burners – one of the most frequently requested features for a country home. Much that would be familiar in a town or a city, such as the provision of heating, power and water, will often require a different and more tailored approach for more remote properties or which have never had access to mains services due to history, geography or investment.

Many buyers we help are retiring and are looking for a slower pace of life, but we increasingly meet people who are looking to relocate to improve the quality of their working lives and to give their children a country upbringing. For them, finding work or setting up and running a business is important, so we've included a chapter on 'Rural businesses and holiday lets'. Many house searches specify a desire to own or run 'holiday lets' too, which is why we have added some insights into this market and included some suggestions to consider when embarking upon such a venture.

For many buyers, country life also offers the chance to live a greener lifestyle, so we've also included a guide to 'The good life', including everything from how to manage footpaths to keeping livestock, alongside a few tips to getting the best out of a vegetable plot.

The British Isles make up a unique patchwork of people and places that have taken thousands of years to form. During over a decade of making *Escape to the Country* we have explored all four nation states; England, Scotland, Wales and Northern Ireland. We have championed their histories and marvelled at their buildings while being immersed in their landscapes. In doing so, patterns have emerged that form the basis for the ten regions we explore in Part II, 'Exploring the British Isles'. Those chosen are the most popular areas for the many hundreds of buyers we have helped over the years as, sadly, there isn't the space in this book to cover everywhere and we will inevitably have left out many captivating and enchanting parts of the UK. Some regions will be familiar but some, I hope, will come as a welcome surprise. I never tire of exploring our countryside, as it always delights and surprises me and creates wonderful memories of people and places that I've been lucky enough to meet and explore. I'm quite certain that if I lived for a century and never stopped travelling around the UK I would still only have scratched the surface, but that is the great joy of living and working in Britain. Its diverse landscapes, and the history that has shaped them, means there is always plenty more to discover.

However, the most important aim is to inspire you to make the move. Country life may not always be easier or cheaper than more urban lifestyles, but in my experience it could be the most rewarding undertaking any of us might make. I therefore invite you to share in what I have learned over many years and take the plunge; the sense of community and the welcome you are sure to find will outweigh almost everything else as you embark on a distinctly new chapter for the future.

PART I
COUNTRY LIFE

'I have been searching for two years for a home in the country and the site is the most beautiful and charming I have ever seen.'
Winston Churchill

This was how Churchill described Chartwell, his own Escape to the Country, when he acquired the property back in the early 1920s. Whether we can afford a country estate or a terraced cottage, or want to settle in glorious isolation or enjoy the delights of a village community, the range of what the countryside can offer is unrivalled. But while the lure of fresh air and open spaces is tangible, is there something more intuitive in our relationship with the countryside that continues to attract, beguile and inspire us?

Throughout a lifetime both living and working in the country, it's a question I have often pondered. My suspicion is that it's a fundamental product of the unique history we all share as Britons. Up until the eighteenth century, when the Industrial Revolution resulted in the rapid expansion and development of our urban centres, most people would have lived in the countryside. Across a relatively underpopulated landscape dotted with small towns, villages, hamlets and farmsteads it afforded us space, land on which to produce food and rear livestock, and offered plenty of raw materials such as timber and stone with which to build a home. In short, as creatures that evolved in the natural world there is undoubtedly something within us that feels at home in the great outdoors, even if just for a few hours. The countryside was, and in many ways remains, the great provider, and there are still some things that even the ardent city dweller can't ignore. The warmth of an open fire taps into something primeval; I challenge anyone not to be transfixed by the sight of dancing flames or soothed by the sweet and timeless smell of wood smoke, while a stunning view can demand a welcome pause for reflection that even the most hectic schedule can't deny.

Chartwell, overlooking the Kentish Weald, was Winston Churchill's lifetime project.

The growth of towns and cities has meant that many of us need to go back many generations to find our rural roots, but rest assured, we will all have them. My experience of working on *Escape to the Country* has provided a fascinating insight into aspirations to 'live the dream'. I have met myriad people in a wealth of places up and down the UK, but while each combination of buyers and properties is unique, there are nonetheless certain common themes that unite them. Understanding these themes may help you too find your ideal Escape to the Country.

CHAPTER 1

Planning your great escape

Selling up and getting ready to move

Once you have decided to move, getting your current home on the market and ready to sell can be one of the most stressful aspects of moving. Achieving the asking price or close to it will have a huge effect on your future budget, so it's worth taking a ruthless approach to what you are selling and how it will appeal to the market. While not everyone will be in a position to update furniture and fittings, excess clutter both inside and out will always detract, and any efforts you can make to freshen up the décor will pay dividends. Outside, tired garden pots full of dead or dying plants, scruffy borders, faded lawns and sheds crammed with junk will all put potential buyers off. Don't forget you are also going to be a buyer, so take every step to market the home you are leaving with a clear determination and sense of pride to ensure that you get as much out of it as you can.

The hunt

There is no such thing as the perfect buyer on *Escape to the Country*. Throughout hundreds of house hunts I can honestly say no two sets of buyers have ever been the same, but they have fallen broadly into two distinct camps. The first are those for whom the chance to live a greener life is paramount; if not quite off-grid they are determined to forge a future with an altogether lighter environmental footprint than ever before, making the best use of the space they have, to live as sustainably as possible.

The second group are in the majority, and it is those for whom the countryside often offers a markedly different type of property than they've had before. Character, kerb appeal, call it what you will, but most will have their heart set on something that is a contrast to what they are moving from. Some will also look to take on a project and we offer some tips on how to go about doing this on page 36.

Where to go, and what to buy?

We are fortunate to live in a country that has a tantalising array of options when it comes to choosing where we might want to live. From the fertile flatlands of East Anglia to the rolling downs of the South East, the open moorland of North Yorkshire, Cumbria or Wales to the mountainous Highlands or the rugged West Coast, we have it all. From picturesque cottages and rambling farmhouses to elegant manors, the wealth of architecture on offer and the rich social and economic history it represents is what makes exploring the countryside such a privilege. The story of our nation is there to read among the pretty lanes and beautiful homes whose architecture characterises the most distinct regions of Britain.

Moving to the country: my top 10 thoughts

1 The countryside is cheaper Not always! Yes, you will often find greater value for money, but the idea that everything is going for a song simply isn't the case. Negotiate sensibly and respectfully. It may be a buyers' market in some areas, but don't think turning up with a pocket full of cash will make you something special. Vendors enjoy selling to people they like; if you want a sensible answer, make a sensible offer. It will go a long way to easing any later negotiations on fixtures and fittings.

2 Beware the holiday romance! I've met plenty of people who've fallen into the trap of wanting to move to a favoured holiday destination, only to find that they can't recapture the fun of a break in the longer term. Holidaying is a great way to get to know an area, but take time to find your way around the practicalities: where is the doctor, the mechanic and the plumber? Where will you buy your food? Does the area have the right amenities such as schools and public transport? If you are planning on working, or running a business, do your research before you commit.

3 Be flexible For obvious reasons, increasing budgets is rarely an option if you can't find what you are looking for.

But you can widen the search area. Don't get too hung up on keeping your search within an hour's drive of this or that. An extra 20–30 minutes on a journey isn't the end of the world if it gets you the kind of home you have longed for. If you can be very flexible, you may want to consider a completely different, and more affordable, area – there are some hidden gems in the UK so keep an open mind.

4 Leave room to improve Odds are, you are going to want to spend some money on your new home. Don't allow your maximum budget to monopolise your search. Keep some funds in reserve to allow for improvements, and search at a lower level, allowing you room to invest in your new rural retreat.

5 Outbuildings I find that these are a factor of many house searches that often take up more time and effort than they deserve. Many of us want outbuildings for workshops, stables, studios or storage, but only viewing properties that already have them can limit your search unnecessarily. Remember, so long as you have space and can obtain the relevant consents, building a suitable outbuilding from scratch may well be a better option in the long run because you will get exactly what you want and, importantly, where you want it in relation to your home.

6 Land Many of us aspire to it, but how many of us really know what to do with it? To the smallholder it's obvious, but for the average family home if you don't need it, don't buy it. With prices around the country for grazing and paddocks ranging from £5,000–15,000 an acre, those few acres on the particulars will chew up a good chunk of your budget. Ask the vendor if there is room to negotiate on price and the amount of land included. It could save you a lot.

7 The Good Life Our increased awareness of food provenance is one of the great draws for anyone moving out of the city. The chance to be self-sufficient is an increasingly popular aim, but it takes time, effort and space to really make it work. If you don't have the money to buy a smallholding, don't despair. Finding land to rent is a realistic way of giving you space without a huge capital investment, and if you find it doesn't work or your situation changes, you can walk away.

8 Transport Getting around is an important consideration; are you ready to get in the car to buy a pint of milk? Village properties with land that are within walking distance of local shops and pubs are particularly hard to find. If you are a drive away from local amenities the trick is to plan ahead, especially during the winter. A good freezer will help! Look into public transport options too – they may not be plentiful but they will disappear altogether if we don't use them.

9 Fuel Running a country home often presents challenges that you are unlikely to encounter in most urban properties. The chances are you won't be on mains gas, although liquefied petroleum gas (LPG) in storage tanks is now widely available, while many rural homes rely on oil for heating and hot water. I'm a huge fan of fuel diversity. At home we run on a range of oil (cooking and heating), wood burners (cooking and heating) and gas (hob), all independent of one another. There is also the opportunity to explore alternative fuel sources (see page 54).

10 'Life in the country is easier!'
The countryside has its advantages, but ease isn't always one of them, particularly if you really do want to live in the middle of nowhere. You need to plan and be organised in terms of your key supplies, be prepared for the weather and you need to be resourceful. Getting things done in a hurry isn't always possible unless you are prepared to, quite literally, do it yourself. In remote spots, grasping basic building and plumbing skills will prove invaluable and can be great fun, adding value and a huge sense of connection to your new home.

Understanding what the many and varied regions of the UK have to offer in terms of their history, culture, architecture and feel is vital when deciding where you want to live. Some decisions are led by a childhood memory of holidays by the sea or up in the hills, while others will see it as the chance to realise a long-held ambition. I also meet many buyers for whom *Escape to the Country* is an opportunity to return to the place where they were born after many years of living and working away.

Of course, often your choice of area is determined by factors such as where you work, proximity to schools and hospitals or other family issues, but I often meet couples who are free of such constraints. If you are lucky enough to enjoy complete freedom of choice as to where you want to live, you could have the pick of the countryside, allowing you to aim for exactly the kind of home you are after.

For most of us it's a happy compromise between enjoying a home the like of which we may never have experienced before, and doing so in an inspiring part of the country, and improving the quality of our lives and our impact on the world around us.

Timber and thatch are an irresistible mix, as seen here in Wiltshire.

The 'property horizon'

Inevitably, budget is usually the most influential factor in determining what you can buy in your chosen area. Different regions have different entry points when it comes to buying a classic *Escape to the Country*-type of property. Taking for example the basic idea of an historic and characterful three-bedroom cottage with a manageable garden in a pretty location, it is possible in the very broadest terms to identify a range of 'property horizons' across the country as a whole.

For example, it means such a cottage in Kent might set you back around £500,000, while the same thing in West Wales or the Scottish Borders may well come in at around half that figure. It is easy to see how areas that have historically been popular with escapees come with the highest price tags, particularly in those counties and regions that have proximity to our largest urban centres such as London, Birmingham and Manchester. Taking London as an example, the surrounding counties of Hertfordshire, Buckinghamshire, Surrey, Sussex, Kent and Essex come with a hefty premium because of their geographic location and popularity with commuters.

The same is also true in those counties that make up the South West such as Wiltshire, Somerset, Dorset and Devon, while the coastal highlights of Cornwall and the long-standing draw of the Cotswolds will also adversely affect how much bang you get for your hard-earned bucks, as will hunting for properties within our National Parks, such as the Lake District. Throughout Part II 'Exploring the British Isles' we offer some alternatives.

Market towns

Many buyers I've met over the years have stumbled because the properties they have seen have, after careful thought, been found to be too far from essential amenities. Regardless of your age, access to doctors, hospitals and even a pint of milk can be of vital importance and with good reason. The older we get the more necessary it is to have these services nearby, while

Gold Hill, in the heart of Shaftesbury in Dorset has, for many of us, come to embody a timeless vision of country life, ever since it shot to fame as the backdrop for the Hovis bread advert in the 1970s.

younger buyers will want the chance to access good schools and the local jobs market. All these factors can be eased if you turn your attention to life in a vibrant market town.

As a taster, Cirencester (Gloucestershire), Buxton (Derbyshire), Shaftesbury (Dorset) or Bury St Edmunds (Suffolk), to name but a very few, provide an idea of what is on offer and what the advantages might be in choosing one of the hundreds of rural towns across the country. My own definition of what makes a good market town includes appealing architecture, a real sense of history with a bustling community that's served with decent transport links to the rest of the country and, of course, easy access to those important facilities, amenities and enticing local countryside. You'll often find that the surrounding area is also packed with other attractions that will serve to both entertain and inspire you and your guests, and which will help to generate a real affinity for your new region and home. When imagining an Escape to the Country you may initially picture splendid isolation, but in truth a large percentage of the buyers I've known would have been well served with a beautiful home in a beautiful town, where the great outdoors is just a short stroll away.

Wherever you decide to go, the fact remains that your choice of location is crucial in determining what kind of country home you are likely to find. If you love oak-framed and thatched properties, don't set your heart on North Wales because they simply don't exist there, but many stunning alternatives do. What's more, falling in love with a particular house is all very well, but it is as important to have a deep affinity with the region or county you are moving to. Identifying with the area that will ultimately have to sustain your new life should be given equal thought from the outset; spending time exploring it before or during your house hunt will never be time wasted, and will almost certainly throw up new perspectives and options, even in those parts of the country you may have thought you knew inside out.

CHAPTER 2

Choosing your country property

Once you have decided *where* you might want to move to, understanding the kind of home you wish to buy is without doubt one of the most important questions that any buyer must confront. Yet despite the best efforts of many people I meet, accurately describing and defining the kind of house that might suit you can be frustratingly difficult.

Homes with 'character' that are 'light and airy' and which offer 'peace and quiet' are descriptions often used on *Escape to the Country*, but such broad headings can be interpreted in numerous different ways. In many respects, it's easier to begin with a list of what you think you don't want, and while many properties I see can change a previously entrenched view as to what not to look for, it does at least provide a starting point. The lessons learned from the viewings should do the rest, provided you remain flexible and are prepared to change your mind over issues that, once overcome, may deliver a property that in all other respects is ideal.

Not surprisingly homes with 'character' are top of everybody's list; I've yet to meet anyone who hasn't sought it, but it is often in the eye of the beholder. It is perfectly possible to find a new-build that is bursting with character such as a modern green-oak gem. At the same time, period properties can just as easily lack that all important 'feel', sometimes because the period features we might expect to find have been misguidedly stripped out in the past.

What makes the perfect house?

This is a question I'm often asked, but in truth what's deemed 'perfect' to one buyer may be anything but to another. Put simply, it comes down to personal taste. While lavish and ingenious finishes may beguile us into thinking a property is somehow perfect I've yet to see one that doesn't, to some degree, require a measure of compromise. My conclusion, having both bought and sold throughout my life, is that the perfect house does exist, but you should seek to define what is perfect to you. To my mind, the perfect house, like the perfect partner, is one which so captures your heart and imagination that it makes you want to forgive and embrace its imperfections, because it just feels right.

An ancient bridge, a babbling brook and a stone cottage: ingredients for the perfect rural home.

With the wealth of property magazines and online resources now available, it is well worth creating a 'mood board' of styles and features that appeal. Much of the housing stock in the UK is over 100 years old, meaning that many of us will have some experience of living in a Victorian home or flat. Georgian properties with their high ceilings and large windows are always popular, while few would argue over the merits of a classic and cosy timber or stone-built cottage. Yet for all the obvious history that forms the foundation of the rural property market, there are now plenty of new-builds that combine the benefits of new materials and building practices with some truly memorable design. I've often shown homes to buyers who were not aware that they favoured one period or style over another until we'd introduced them to it. Mood boards are a brilliant way of helping you identify what it is you are looking for, even if you aren't familiar with specific architectural terms.

House DNA

One of the main reasons we succeed in helping so many on *Escape to the Country* is the skill and intuition we have developed in understanding what our buyers are looking for. This may seem obvious, but all too often an estate agent's view of what a buyer *wants* is restricted to location, number of bedrooms and budget. However, we go into great detail in profiling the very specific *needs* of our buyers. The result is what might be likened to a DNA bar code, which we then seek to match to the corresponding bar code a property might offer. The result is rarely a perfect match, but it is enough to introduce buyers to what should broadly be the right property in the right place at the right price. The aim as always is to find a house that not only caters for their very particular family needs, but which also inspires an emotional attachment over and above the obvious wow factor.

Buying an old house

In an age when we have become addicted to having everything we buy being brand new, beautifully packaged and coming with a guarantee, buying property can present an uncomfortable contradiction. The rural property market tends to be dominated with older properties that come with no such modern reassurances; in effect, if an older property is for you, it's akin to spending several hundred thousand pounds in a charity shop on a second-hand item that you hope will last a lifetime.

I have met many buyers who've been confounded by this conundrum, who at the end of a house search, having seen various traditional properties have diverted their ambitions towards a new-build – often seeking what they already have, albeit in a more rural location.

There is no firm rule as to what you should buy – so long as it works for you. However, older properties do tend to come with the sort of history, character and style that most of us seek precisely because they have evolved over time, reflecting the different needs and tastes of generations of owners.

Old houses should therefore be approached with an open mind but with some care as to what you may be taking on.

- Don't view older properties if you can't cope with the sorts of foibles you are likely to find, such as wonky walls or uneven floors.
- Don't buy something that's the wrong size; if your prospective house is governed by listing or conservation issues, you may not be able to extend it.
- Always have a detailed survey carried out, and make sure your budget can cope with any alterations or repairs you may wish to make. Pay particular attention to roofs, wiring, plumbing and heating, as well as any possible damp issues or history of flooding.

Country house guide

I never cease to be inspired by the range of properties the countryside has to offer, and marvel at the great number that have survived centuries of history. From those that have been around for hundreds of years to modern avant-garde designs, the architectural wealth of Britain's rural property market is without doubt one of the main reasons that *Escape to the Country* is now enjoyed in over 30 countries around the world.

Over its lifetime, the series has become a great ambassador for the British countryside and its rich social and architectural history. The legacy of the British Empire saw much of what we take for granted in our landscape and villages exported overseas as the nation's imperial ambitions soared in the eighteenth and nineteenth centuries. From the weather-boarded mansions and cottages of the American east coast, and even the Presidential White House, to the grand Neo-classical public buildings of the Far East, all can trace their roots back to buildings built in Britain over the last 500 years or so.

Cottages

To most of us the humble cottage is the epitome of country living. My own first property was a wonderful stone cottage in the hills of Mid Wales and doing it up set me on a path that changed my life forever. Of course, many these days aren't as humble as when first built. Improved and extended over centuries in some cases, cottages can command high prices in hotspots such as the Cotswolds or on the coast, but wherever they are, the best examples should combine appealing architecture, history and that all-important character with classic features, such as working fireplaces, exposed beams and a beautiful setting.

Although usually lacking the open-plan living space that many families desire, at the right price cottages can still be great options for growing families albeit with some compromise. They may challenge your need for upstairs storage for example. It is worth remembering that when first built, a classic cottage was never lived in by a family with lots of possessions; farmworkers simply did not have the need for cavernous wardrobes. While these days many have been redesigned downstairs to provide a welcoming kitchen-diner, living room and possibly a spacious garden room, what you gain on the ground floor you tend to lose on the first. What's more, many conversions and renovations will have removed any original loft space to gain ceiling height. That said, losing a loft, in my opinion, is no bad thing – most of what's in them tends to be forgotten about for years, so if you can create a storage solution using shelving and clear plastic boxes in an outbuilding the chances are it will be far more accessible and may even tempt you to live with less.

We often talk of compromise when showing houses, and storage in cottages in one of the recurring factors, but if you too relish the chance to live in an historic property that's built from local materials with quirky ceilings, cosy snugs and framed with a pretty garden, they are an absolute dream and always much sought after. They will also feature heavily in any search that seeks to find a home within a village setting.

No other type of building as readily reflects an area's vernacular style as the cottage. Built from whatever was most locally available, they reveal distinctive architectural styles that define many of the UK's most popular rural regions. Clockwise from above: Yew Tree Farm at Coniston, Cumbria; the Walled Garden at Llanerchaeron, Wales; cottages in Grassington, North Yorkshire; the south front of Townend in Troutbeck, Cumbria.

Farmhouses

Farmhouses are a feature of the landscape that developed long after the cottage had established itself in the villages and hamlets of England. A product of the collapse of feudalism when tenants became free to own land of their own, throughout the sixteenth and seventeenth centuries this growing class of landed-farmer saw their holdings and their homes grow through marriage or land purchase. The farmhouse, as we now know it, today occupies a swathe of the rural property market, and not surprisingly they come in all sorts of shapes and sizes, while often representing the best of local vernacular architecture.

Since the Second World War, farms themselves have often seen dramatic changes in size. Many have expanded as mechanisation has encouraged the creation of bigger and more efficiently worked fields, a process which led to the incorporation of numerous smaller holdings of land. Across the UK, perhaps most notably in our arable heartlands such as East Anglia, huge commercial farms of three or four thousand acres are now not uncommon, but the result has been that many original farmhouses themselves have become surplus to requirements and have been sold off, usually with a very manageable handful of acres surrounding them. The result has been to introduce to the rural market some truly beautiful properties that have evolved over time with rambling layouts, period features and outbuildings, making for some of the most desirable houses on offer.

The country kitchen

Most buyers we help have a spacious country kitchen at the top of their wish list. The once humble kitchen has developed into the central feature of any home, somewhere in which to both cook and entertain, with a modern open-plan kitchen-diner now the most sought after feature in properties across the country.

The modern kitchen is a response to the way we live today, but when it comes to rural homes, it was the evolution of the farmhouse kitchen that took the lead as a design classic.

Traditionally the farmhouse kitchen was very much the heart of agricultural life. It was here that bread was baked, washing boiled, baths taken and food prepared for the family and a wide array of farm workers. A cast-iron range of the sort that came into being during the Victorian period was central to this activity and in subsequent years it has become

I'm a huge fan of using a mix of freestanding and other units to create a kitchen that combines different materials and textures as well as practicality, and which also gives a flavour of the characters and personalities that use it. Few rooms reveal as much about who we are and the kind of life we lead as our kitchens.

A classic range (below right) provides an iconic focal point, while (above right) the modern taste for more light and space combines traditional materials in these stunning new-builds from Border Oak.

a focal point for many kitchens, epitomised since the 1920s in the form of the Aga, Esse and the like.

Ideally square in shape, the best farmhouse kitchen will accommodate a large kitchen table and chairs, somewhere from which day-to-day life can be run and enjoyed. Over the years, we have seen some lavish examples complete with abundant storage, in beautifully crafted units, often coming at an eye-watering cost. Yet there is a timeless appeal in those that can combine the best of fitted practicality around sinks and cookers, with the effortless charm of free-standing furniture, giving a kitchen its personality and texture, providing a rich and warm welcome. Of all the features that will clinch a sale, a stunning kitchen is undoubtedly top of the list but with imagination and ingenuity it need not cost the earth, even if it may look as if it has. In my experience the best have been achieved more through creative flair and a passion for design, rather than an open-ended chequebook.

These manor houses with Georgian windows and graceful lines exude a timeless style and presence all their own. Both are listed, but easily combine modern amenities with historic charm.

Manors and rectories

The manor house, as we know it, is a product of the late medieval period, when the country seats of the nobility were transformed from fortified strongholds to comfortable and graceful homes that began to celebrate architectural design and demonstrate the social standing of their owners, a transition perhaps exemplified in many Tudor and Elizabethan properties. Traditionally the manor house was the centre of a noble's estate or manor, which varied in size. Some might have included several villages or hamlets, and evolved into the great estates of the eighteenth and nineteenth centuries. This new post-medieval style of building reflected not only a more peaceful social and

political landscape, but also defined their owners as a growing middle class of gentry whose prosperity owed more to increasing trade and commerce, than military conquest or the benevolence of the monarch. There is nothing quite like a classic Georgian manor house to charge the aspirations of house hunters, yet there are plenty of other stunning examples, untouched by the eighteenth-century craze for Neo-classical design. The rich, honey-coloured stone of the Cotswolds was used to build some of the finest, while the Victorians too made the genre their own with lavish use of red-brick and slate, a common sight on the Welsh Borders and into Cheshire.

Historic rectories also occupy a very particular and appealing slice of the rural market. Built for the clergy at a time when their positions were often managed and endowed by significant local landowners, the properties they were provided with often saw no expense spared. Architecturally many were based upon the style of the estates they stood in, designed to be viewed as conspicuous extensions of the generous benefaction of their sponsors, a far cry from the modern versions now put up by the church itself. As a member of society's upper tier, the buildings they enjoyed were usually of a size that would accommodate not just the vicar and his family, but a modest clutch of servants too, set within good surroundings close to the church itself, locations that are easy to spot these days. Over many years we have seen some fantastic examples of these well-built and sometimes brooding buildings, those put up during the Victorian period being among some of the best.

Smallholdings

The smallholding is often seen by those seeking a greener lifestyle as the perfect solution; they provide a modest amount of land with which to attempt a degree of sustainability, but without the burden and costs of taking on a full-scale farm. Typically between 5 and 40 acres in size, smallholdings offer the scope to rotate land use and develop a classic mixed system of agriculture, which can sustain a range of livestock and arable production that is reminiscent of the days when smaller family farms were commonplace in the countryside. West Wales is a good option for smallholders, where smaller farms, or those which have already been turned into smallholdings, are available and can be more affordable than elsewhere.

However, finding a property with the right amount of land can necessitate some compromise on the property that comes with it. Affordability of land can be an indicator of rural areas that have historically struggled economically. Over the years, I have seen many such properties that have been successfully improved and extended to become beautiful and practical homes. What's more, because they come with land, they can also allow the enterprising smallholder the chance of diversifying into other income-generating initiatives. Lately, glamping and other forms of holiday let (such as yurts or shepherd's huts) have become popular options, and creating retreats for yoga or creative pursuits are some of the ways in which land can be made to pay its way and recoup the costs of buying it in the first place.

Digging your veg beds is a task always made easier with some help and a well-earned break.

Chapel conversions

The converted chapel is a unique style of property that has increased in popularity over the last 30 years or so. Not to be confused with converted churches, which are rarer and which tend to come with the complicated issue of graveyards, the vast majority of chapels are splendid buildings ranging in size from the very modest to huge structures, which can dominate their surroundings. Most were built to satisfy congregations of Methodists, Lutherans and other non-conformists, and while many may still contain plaques and dedications on their walls, most don't have the problem of surrounding graveyards. Large numbers are also to be found in the hearts of many villages with the added bonus of having community right on the doorstep. One issue with village settings can be that such chapels lack gardens, however I've seen many situated in more isolated positions with sizeable pieces of land, giving them excellent gardens and parking spaces, along with room for sheds and other outbuildings.

Common across the UK, they are particularly abundant in Wales but you'll also find large numbers in Cumbria, Yorkshire and Cornwall. Regardless of denomination, what most share is their age; the majority tending to have been built during Britain's building heyday of the mid- to late nineteenth century. Victorian ingenuity and striking architectural features often combine to provide some stunning living spaces that make clever use of details such as windows, pillars, balconies, supporting corbels and vaulted ceilings, while the chances are you'll get a solid front door with a giant wrought-iron key that won't fit in your pocket.

Church conversion. While chapel conversions are relatively easy to find, churches are much rarer due to the governance of the Church of England. However, some have been sold off for conversion, such as this fabulous example in Somerset.

Barns

Of all the properties we showcase on *Escape to the Country*, barn conversions are some of the most sought after. Since the end of the Second World War, the trend for renovating and converting them has accelerated. With flare, and an eye for celebrating their original design and purpose, huge numbers have today been turned into what are often very spacious domestic homes. This dramatic and welcome repurposing followed a wholesale change in farming practice that now demands much bigger and more easily maintained farm buildings capable of housing larger numbers of livestock and much bigger items of farm machinery. The result is that many farms have successfully sold off their smaller barns to developers or individuals to create fantastic living spaces imbued with striking features while combining the very best of modern contemporary design.

By definition, the location of barns within the countryside usually gives them a stunning setting, while an increasing number of redundant farmyards has tempted many to develop what was once a busy collection of dairies, grain stores and stables into beautiful complexes that offer several unique properties within a ready-made community of owners.

Architecturally they often reflect an area's vernacular style that betrays much about a region's economic and material history. In areas without a natural source of stone they tend to be large timber-framed structures with cavernous glazed central entrance halls, which would once have accommodated tall carts and horses. Some of the best examples can be found in the timber-framed heartlands of East Anglia, the Kent Weald and Sussex while in the West Country, Wales and the Cotswolds great stone-built barns are sought after by those keen to transform them into spacious family homes. No two are ever the same, while in areas where livestock farming has been the principal agricultural regime, such as Wales, the Peak District, Yorkshire and Cumbria, many smaller examples built from distinctive local stone now feature in the property market.

Mill conversions

The interest in converting what were once very undomestic buildings into homes is perhaps no better demonstrated than in the often-ingenious approach taken to developing old mills. Windmills, of course, bring their own challenges in terms of space and the demands of vertical living. The most successful of these will almost certainly have an added ground-floor extension providing reception, kitchen and dining areas more amenable to modern life, while retaining the unmistakable tower as bedroom space. Some notable examples I've seen have removed the sails and the gear, replacing them with an upper floor that offers 360-degree views of the surrounding countryside. When it comes to a mystery house, there is nothing quite like a windmill.

Watermills, however, can offer their enterprising owners the additional incentive and benefit of generating their own power thanks to the source of water that runs either around or underneath it. Over the years, I have seen many that have created striking living spaces, making much of the original

We discovered this eye-catching mill conversion in Cornwall. It came with a memorable water feature: its restored and working overshot wheel.

mill-workings that many have retained as unique and memorable architectural features.

New-builds

It is a common misconception that *Escape to the Country* demands that you buy a period property. While for most the opportunity to live in a home full of history and character can be the driving force behind their move, for many others it can also provide the chance to step into a building that offers a country life without the need to maintain something more traditional. Many successful renovations result in what is effectively a brand-new home that conforms to modern standards and regulations in terms of maintenance and energy efficiency, but makes the most of the original building shell that surrounds it.

Something old, something new

Moira and David's Escape to the Country eventually led them to a property unlike anything they'd originally planned for.

Regardless of the success of a house search, the process always leaves our buyers with a clearer idea of what they are looking for. In the summer of 2018, I joined David and Moira from Swindon who'd asked us to help find them a new home in Leicestershire so they could move closer to their children and grandchildren. The brief was clear; they wanted an older property in a village location that had been well renovated with as much character as possible, ideally with enough land to have a pony or two for the newest and smallest members of their expanding family.

With three properties to see, the first enjoying the merits of a recent

It was a journey of trial and error, but in the end David and Moira, seen here with their grandson Harry, were delighted with their new home.

renovation, and then a seventeenth-century gem, the search was going well. However, our mystery house, a new-build within sight of Belvoir Castle near Grantham, so caught their imagination that they put in an offer. Unfortunately, the deal fell through, but the whole experience threw up some important lessons.

Undeterred, they soon began a new search, but with a completely different focus; yes, they still wanted a characterful house, but they were now prepared to entertain new-builds specifically because of the space and finish they might provide, and they were far more flexible as to the location. Within a couple of months, they found their perfect home; a sprawling, recently completed property that had all the space they needed, both inside and out, set in 3 acres. The house was also just over the border in Lincolnshire, and just half an hour away from the mystery house they had originally sought to buy.

In the early summer of 2019 I was keen to see what they had bought and what they had learnt. David was clear about the merits of looking at as many properties as possible to finally understand what it is you are looking for. 'You've got to be flexible, and that's what we learnt from our house hunt with you.' For Moira, the experience was also profound: 'If we hadn't taken part in *Escape to the Country* we'd never have looked at a house like this. We were insistent on age and character, and that had blinkered our previous search. I grew up in older properties and was convinced that's what we wanted, but opening our eyes to the obvious merits of a new-build led us through the door of this one.'

A year on, and they could not be happier. For their first Christmas, their children had a new door sign made that wryly serves to remind everyone who visits of the journey that finally brought them to their new home; 'Not the Mystery House'!

A good sense of humour and an open mind are key ingredients to successful house hunting.

New-builds of course come in myriad shapes and sizes. While it is true that a good number are, by any measure, architecturally bland, I've also seen some stunning examples that have been designed and sited to make much of a view and their position relative to the sun. Many too have also successfully combined a flavour of the local traditional architecture with inspiring modern materials and ideas.

Building from scratch also affords the possibility of creating homes that have been conceived with a battery of eco or green credentials. From solar heating and hot water, to air and ground source heat pumps, many also have an aspect that can capitalise on what architects call 'solar gain'. Put simply, large glazed areas giving access to panoramic windows, or bifold doors that lead out to a garden, can have the added benefit of effortlessly harnessing the heat of the sun. These additions have a huge impact on heating costs, and current building regulations will ensure that your new home is as well insulated as possible. The result is that the good new-build will often give you a striking home that should sit within the landscape as well as something more traditional, and which will be cheaper to run, while at the same time representing yet another chapter in our rural architectural history.

Mystery houses

Of all the elements that make up an episode of *Escape to the Country*, without doubt the most anticipated is our pick of the Mystery House. Since the series was first conceived, this eclectic offering has evolved into a favourite with both buyers and the wider audience. In essence, it is a chance to showcase a region's finest and most unusual property within the financial and other parameters we've been given. Yet its success in harvesting sales is much more nuanced. Every home we show must provide our buyers with a viable solution to their wish-list, but in truth many people struggle to accurately describe the kind of home they want. Our selection of mystery houses uses our experience and intuition to sense what it is our buyers are after, and gives us the chance to tempt them with something that meets their demands but in a way that perhaps they won't have considered before.

Finding the perfect mystery house may mean we have to step outside the prescribed envelope in terms of location, style and, to some extent budget, but the best examples will always sell themselves and be a complement to the other properties we have shown.

In choosing our mystery houses, arresting and unusual architecture that remains true to the needs of our buyers is crucial. Converted windmills are always a favourite.

Over the years, we have been able to reveal manor houses, windmills and watermills, converted barns and chapels, Grade I-listed Elizabethan gems and even a medieval tower. Not surprisingly many buyers often willingly reconsider their original must-haves on their wish-list, many of which evaporate when set against the stunning and unique buildings, which our mystery houses seek to champion.

Outbuildings

Outbuildings that might lend themselves to overspill domestic accommodation, office space, studios, stables or workshops are high on many buyers' wish-lists.

However, while many may need improvement, renovating them can prove more expensive than building from new, depending on what it is you want them for. That said, a beautiful stone barn will clearly appeal to many and with good reason. Combining character and the chance to put your stamp on a forlorn outbuilding are all good reasons to renovate, as is the chance to make much of quirky historic features such as you'd find in an old stable range or forge.

But beware the trap of only searching for properties that already have an outbuilding. This can unnecessarily limit the scope of a house hunt, whereas if you find an existing property with enough outdoor space you may find that designing something from scratch will give you exactly what you want, where you want it, particularly if you have a view to make much of. In terms of costs, the sky really is the limit, from simple sectional sheds and workshops to lavish oak-framed structures. Building anything new will usually require permission, not least if it's within the shadow of a listed property, so if the provision of an outbuilding for whatever purpose is a deal breaker, it's probably worth consulting with the local planning authority and conservation officers before you buy.

In a world which demands we buy everything brand new, the character that comes with most historic properties is often priceless. This original window, lined with an artist's pots and brushes conjures the romance of an artisan escape.

Country gardens

Making a house a home is all very well, but when it comes to country property it is often nothing without a garden. Large or small, landscaped or managed wilderness, the garden of any rural retreat is the frame that sets it off. We'd expect an expensive painting to have a beautiful frame so why not our home? Sadly, I often see wonderful houses that are let down by the absence of any care or consideration for their outside space. Not only does it take away from the house itself, it also makes it much harder to sell on to a buyer who may not have the imagination or will to give it the makeover it needs.

For many escapees, particularly those planning a bolthole from the urban sprawl, the chance to have a sizeable and useful garden, possibly for the first time in their lives, is one of the principal factors driving a move. The wish for vegetable plots and the opportunity to attempt a degree of productive self-sufficiency is a common ambition, but so too is the chance to have outdoor space for living and relaxing in, overlooked by nothing but the peace and quiet of the landscape and its wildlife.

Gardening is famously only what you make of it, and while I'm a keen gardener myself, I understand that for many it's a chore they don't relish despite their obvious appreciation of a garden done well. Yet creating a space that does justice to the property it envelops need not be a problem. Clever, low maintenance designs and materials grace many of the finest and most extensive gardens, while containers and trellised climbers can make the very best of smaller plots and courtyards.

The walled gardens of our greatest country houses were the ultimate solution to producing vast quantities of fantastic fruit and vegetables all year round, but few of us could afford to create one now. Nonetheless many of the skills the walled gardeners of the past developed, and which have been revived in some of the most spectacular examples today, provide valuable insight into getting the best from more modest vegetable gardens and glasshouses.

If gardening is for you, then the opportunity to transform an empty acre or two is the chance of a lifetime – and I say that as someone who was lucky enough to do just that in my first house in Mid Wales 20 years ago. If it's not, don't buy a burden; buy something with a small plot, perhaps with a view beyond the garden that you can enjoy while someone else does the work! Buy not just what you can afford but also what you can manage. I've known house sales fall through because at the eleventh hour the buyers got cold feet over maintaining the beautiful garden the house came with and which ironically helped sell it to them in the first place. Likewise, if you find the right house but the garden is lacking, there is no shame in getting professional and practical help to transform it. Done well, it will not only add to the value of your home, it will also give you a priceless feeling of well-being.

Above: Since the mid-nineteenth century, when Joseph Paxton set about creating affordable glasshouses for the masses, the greenhouse – as we now know it – has become a staple of the country garden.

Left: This cottage garden, with its riot of classic herbaceous plants, offers a quintessential image of country life.

CHAPTER 3

Taking on a project

For many of us, there can be no more fulfilling way to register the change from one lifestyle to another than by taking on a renovation project. Having spent most of my adult life doing just that I can assure you of the rewards, both spiritual and practical, but you should be aware that it really isn't for the faint-hearted!

We often regard renovation as the way to 'make something your own' and that 'transforming a blank canvas' will allow you to 'put your own stamp on it'. This is all true, but if you struggle to bang in a straight nail, think very carefully before you embark on such a venture. That said, you don't need to be a DIY genius, but you should at least have a practical aptitude to help you understand the processes involved so that you can sensibly project-manage the work of others.

There are also potential financial advantages in taking on a renovation project alongside the opportunity to create the home you've dreamed of. The chances are it will be more affordable than if it has been renovated in the past, and there is no guarantee of the quality of previous renovation work. There is nothing quite as comforting as revelling in the knowledge that the craftspeople you've employed have done the best job possible, particularly when it comes to the potential hazards of ancient plumbing and wiring.

Despite the increased interest in renovation, plenty of examples still exist across the country that are in need of long-overdue TLC.

Getting hands on: deciding to reveal this lost fireplace in my home was definitely a challenge …

… but the results just a few weeks later were well worth the sweat and tears, and gave us a cosy snug and a family space with a renewed purpose.

What to look for

From the outset, it's important to understand what you are taking on. What might look like a cosmetic makeover could in time reveal itself to be far more involved, meaning you might incur hefty additional costs. If in any doubt, you should always commission a detailed survey from an expert, preferably one experienced in the type of property you have chosen, and if necessary involve an architect. Alternatively, consider showing it to a recommended builder before you buy. Choose a local builder, preferably one that's likely to do the job for you, as they can offer very practical advice on costs, timescale and design options. Local builders and architects will also help you navigate the planning process if permission is needed, while an architect could be invaluable if you need listed building consent or your project requires significant structural alterations.

Plan your schedule of works with your builder. You may not have the resources to do it all at once (I never have) but the key to a successful project is in making sure you do what needs to be done in the right order; there is no point rushing in and laying a new floor if you are going to have to rip it up two years later when you re-plumb or re-wire.

I've always felt that there are two main criteria to consider with any renovation: what *must* be done to make your home

watertight and address issues that affect its structural integrity; and what you would *like* to do, for example putting in that hand-made kitchen or garden room you've long been hoping for.

Conservation versus renovation

Many of the older properties we see while house hunting have been significantly improved in recent years. Structural alterations, extensions and upgraded or updated services such as plumbing and wiring are reassuring features of many successful renovation projects, but every renovation is only as good as the skills employed in doing it. This is particularly important when thinking of buying a listed building that has had work done in the past as the materials and quality of work will be key to compliance with relevant consents.

If you are thinking of taking on a relatively new building, for example a post-war property, the original build and materials used will be familiar to most local builders and should not present too many challenges, provided your ambitions are structurally sensible. If in doubt always take the advice of an architect or structural engineer.

However, if you are keen to transform and upgrade a period property, you may need to seek out building professionals with more specific skills. My first house was a traditional stone-built cottage, and required a good understanding, on the part of the builders, of working with rough stone and how it goes together. With our current home, we had to start again in understanding the very specific demands of a solid-walled, timber-framed house and the kinds of artisan skills needed to work with oak, lathes and lime plaster, with the additional demands of obtaining the right consents to renovate a listed building.

It is at this point that many renovations must step into the world of conservation. The use of building-specific materials that follow the principles of breathability are one aspect; questions must also be asked whether it is better to replace or repair a feature, all of which need careful consideration.

This may all sound onerous, but the business of improving and extending the life of an historic building is hugely rewarding, and the process of understanding traditional skills and practices such as lime-work, stonemasonry and thatching is, in my experience, fascinating. Happily, there has been a resurgence of people training in these skills and you will find a network of talented craftspeople up and down the country.

What to consider before taking on a project

- Make sure you are aware of the starting point. A detailed assessment of the current condition of your home will help to prevent any nasty surprises later, so invest in the necessary expert surveys.
- Assess the work in detail with the help of a builder or architect based upon what has to be done (for example, re-roofing) against what you'd like to do (adding or extending). Ensure you have the right permissions and consents from your planning department, and if it's listed, your conservation officer.
- Plan a detailed schedule of works so that you do what needs to be done in the right order. Then plan it all again to make sure it's realistic and reliable. You may not be able to afford to do it all at once, so phasing your work appropriately will be key to making the process as efficient as possible and keeping the costs down.
- Costing. Working to a budget is critical, but you should make allowances for an overspend, particularly if you are dealing with an older property that may reveal more issues as you work through it, despite your best efforts to be prepared. When our plumber started to run the new pipes through the house for our central heating system, we found that one of our floors was completely rotten so the plumbing work had to stop while that was replaced.
- Get the right team together. There are plenty of building firms and architects that will project manage the whole thing for you, or you could manage it yourself (we did). Either way, finding the right team is always best achieved through local recommendation. We have also found that combining the roles of plumber and electrician in one person is a definite advantage; they can map out the schedule of these essential fixes with your builder ensuring time isn't wasted.
- We've always taken the view that our builders work with us, not for us. Establishing a good and constructive relationship with a team you trust and who will share in your vision is essential in ensuring its timely completion, while also allowing them to add their own flair and suggestions to what you have asked them to craft.

Beam cleaning

Many period properties have had their timber beams painted or stained over the years. In some instances, tar was applied to external beams to protect them; in others limewash was used. Many houses have also had their internal beams painted black, a practice that does little to celebrate the true nature of a beautiful piece of timber. Left untreated, oak will usually revert to a soft honey or silver colour and it has become common practice to remove paint and other finishes to reveal the real colour and texture beneath. Various companies now offer beam-cleaning services using chemicals applied directly to the surface, by blasting them with an abrasive medium at high pressure, or using gentler dry-ice blasting techniques. However, it is worth seeking expert advice from a conservationist or historic building specialist when thinking about cleaning beams, as some of the methods advertised can cause great damage. Moreover, you should beware of companies that claim to restore the natural look of your beams with 'specialist' treatments. These can be nothing more than a theatrical makeover involving painting the surface to make it look original. Remember that as an organic material wood needs to breathe and over-painting will only make the problem worse and could cause more lasting damage.

Alternative power sources

Country life can offer the chance of improving your green credentials when it comes to day-to-day essentials like power and heating. Alternatives now exist to the more traditional options of oil and gas. Both ground and air source heat pumps which rely on electricity can prove effective but only in properties that themselves are thermally efficient; often running at a constant low heat they are great at maintaining temperature levels using underfloor heating, provided your home isn't leaking hot air like a sieve (see page 53).

If you are renovating a project, it's worth thinking about the limitations and advantages of installing modern systems such as these from the outset, particularly if you are able to insulate your home as you renovate it.

The range of what constitutes a project is huge. For some it's a wholesale rebuild, for others it's little more than replacing a kitchen or bathroom or knocking through a wall. Whatever the scope of your abilities or ambitions, rest assured that investing in creating the space you want for your future will give you the kind of reward and connection to your new home that only such effort can bring. As has been said before, if the perfect house is the one which makes you want to embrace its imperfections, tweaking those imperfections you've identified really will help you make it your own, and may well maximise the return on your investment.

Few elements of an historic building relay its pedigree as do a web of interconnected timber joints and beams, displaying the craft and skill of its builders.

CHAPTER 4

Listed buildings

Categories

There are three main categories of listed property, which reflect the historic importance of the building concerned. In England and Wales a grading system is used, while in Scotland it's broken down into categories A, B and C, but they all roughly correspond.

For obvious geographic reasons, the majority are in England, and are graded as follows:

Grade I (2.5 per cent) are buildings of exceptional interest, for example Buckingham Palace, or the Forth Road Bridge in Scotland, which is a corresponding Category A structure.

Grade II* (5.5 per cent) are buildings of particular interest such as Hill Top in Cumbria, now owned by the National Trust but formerly the home of Beatrix Potter.

Grade II (92 per cent) are of special interest and represent most listed properties likely to be seen on the open market.

Few types of homes elicit such extreme opinions as those that, because of their age, architectural style or position, have been listed, so protecting their historic or other merits. Every year I meet many buyers who deliberately avoid listed buildings due to misconceptions about the burden that listing may bring.

My own view, and I say this as the proud owner of a listed property, is that most listed buildings will offer you character, history and a location that make them homes that are a privilege to own. Conversely it follows that if you deliberately avoid listed buildings your choice becomes more limited, and the chances of finding a home that provides for something architecturally memorable will greatly diminish.

I've found that one of the underlying reasons for people avoiding listed buildings is a belief that the listing means domestic life as we know it will stop amid a raft of rules and restrictions. So, it is perhaps worth setting out the facts and busting a few of the myths that surround this unique and valuable slice of the property market.

Listing marks and celebrates a building's special architectural and historic interest, and also brings it under the consideration of the planning system so that it can be protected for future generations… Listing is not a preservation order, preventing change. It does not freeze a building in time, it simply means that listed building consent must be applied for in order to make any changes to that building which might affect its special interest.

HISTORIC ENGLAND

Britain's long and fascinating history has left us with many historic buildings and other monuments, which together describe our nation's story. At the end of the Second World War the risk to many such historic assets was recognised in the 1947 Town and Country Planning Act, which for the first time incorporated a 'List' of significant properties that should be further protected from damage and demolition. Today, the National Heritage List for England (NHLE) is the only official record of properties currently afforded this enhanced protection, while in Wales and Scotland details are held by CADW and Historic Environment Scotland respectively. The List itself expanded rapidly throughout the 1980s during the widespread development boom, such that there are now nearly 500,000 historic buildings and monuments recorded, with significant others added each year. Once a building has been listed, any repairs or alterations required or desired may require permission (consent), which is granted by your local authority, specifically by your conservation officer who will be based in the planning department.

The law and what it means

In broad terms, the law splits changes to listed properties into two key areas; *repairs*, which don't usually require consent, and *alterations*, which do.

The majority of listed properties I've seen offered for sale have undergone considerable renovation and improvement over the years, meaning that much of the perceived hassle has already been taken care of. Nonetheless it's important to understand that whatever changes have been made should have been undertaken with the right consents. You should see

evidence of this before buying, because as the new owner you could still be liable for alterations that occurred in the past, if they were made without relevant permission.

The safeguarding of listed buildings is in the hands of your planning department, specifically your conservation officer. Their aim is to balance the need to protect the historic value of your property, while at the same time being mindful of the need to allow it to evolve and be equipped for modern life. In my experience, most conservation officers are extremely helpful and pragmatic, provided what you're asking for is sensible and sensitive to the historic fabric of the property. New doorways, kitchens, windows, extensions or garden rooms are all possible provided you are prepared to work with your conservation department and remain focused on the best interests of the building and its surroundings.

Like many legal guidelines, those that govern listed buildings can occasionally swirl into grey areas; what to some

The great joy of a listed building is that almost by definition it will have the sort of history, character and period style that most of us are looking for.

is a simple and permitted *repair* may in effect become an *alteration* requiring consent. If you have any doubt as to whether your plans require consent you should always seek it, as it's far better to undertake work within the law and with the right permissions than to claim ignorance later and potentially foot the bill to reverse what you've done. What's more, you may have fundamentally damaged an important historic building, which could lead to prosecution, a hefty fine or, in extreme cases, a custodial sentence.

What you can and can't do

Every year I meet buyers who worry that everything from changing a light bulb to replacing a kitchen or bathroom might be subject to a set of draconian rules that will get in the way of improvement or development.

In trying to offer an easy guide to what you can and can't do to a listed building it's important to remember that each case is specific to the property concerned and there is rarely a one-size-fits-all answer. However, there are some themes and questions that always come up during visits to listed properties up and down the country. To shed light on the most important ones, I asked Peter Bell from the Listed Property Owners' Club (LPOC) to share his thoughts. The LPOC offers an advice service to its members and it's an invaluable resource. It also lobbies government on behalf of listed property owners and has established itself as a highly respected voice in the planning system and wider world of building conservation. Peter also offers a list of dos and don'ts when considering buying a listed property (see p.45).

Can I change the PVC windows or put them in?

There are some great PVC windows on the market today but they will not enhance the value or improve the appearance of your listed building. Listed buildings are special because they use traditional materials and traditional techniques. Installing PVC windows in a listed building would be akin to putting a stainless steel leg on a Chippendale table.

Can I change an historic front door or replace a modern one for old?

Changing the front door can also alter the character and appearance of a building so it needs careful consideration. For a period or historic door it is likely that it will need to be repaired rather than replaced; for a modern door there may well be scope to replace it. Look for one that matches the period of the door opening or the elevation in which it sits.

Can I put in extra doors or windows?

Adding doors and windows will require listed building consent so this needs to be considered carefully. Some elevations are not sensitive to this sort of change but in others, such as the front of a symmetrical Georgian home, it may be out of the question.

Can I install skylights or roof lights into a loft space?

Roof lights on rear or concealed roof slopes of listed buildings are often granted listed building consent. They are likely to be more acceptable if they are not too large, they do not cut through ancient roof timbers and if the number is limited to just one or two depending on the area of the roof.

Can I change the colour of the walls?

Colour is very much a matter of personal choice. There are a few situations in which consent is required to change the colour of walls, such as if there is an historic paint scheme, or the proposed colours are particularly strident. However, most do not require consent. Don't forget that it is important to maintain breathability in the choice of paint, such as clay- or lime-based options. Carefully check the specifications of the product first. Most modern emulsion paints are not breathable and have the same effect as wrapping your wall or home in cling-film, retaining moisture and inviting trouble.

Opposite above: Repair or restoration is usually favoured for windows in listed buildings. Opposite below: Grade I-listed Goddards House in York, built in the Arts and Crafts style.

Can I fix the guttering?

Keeping the gutters and downpipes in good repair is one of the most important areas of routine maintenance that will ensure your building stays in good condition. Cast-iron guttering will last a lifetime if it is well maintained.

Can I install central heating?

There are occasions when a new central heating boiler, new radiators or underfloor heating may require listed building consent. If in doubt speak with the local planning authority or take professional advice. Always make sure that your fitter is aware that the building is listed and that care needs to be taken when positioning the pipe runs and fittings.

Can I change a bathroom suite?

In exceptional circumstances, historic bathroom fittings may contribute to the significance of a listed building, so alterations would require consent. However, in most other circumstances changing the bathroom fittings does not alter the character of the listed building so it can go ahead without consent. If the change involves knocking through an historic wall and requires a new or altered soil vent stack or extractor vent you may need consent for these particular elements.

Can I install an en-suite?

It is often possible to accommodate an en-suite within an existing box room or in a redundant space within a listed building. They will often require new door openings or new partitions so listed building consent will be required but most listed buildings on the market will have had facilities added in recent years.

Can I replace the kitchen?

Replacing the kitchen fittings is not normally an alteration that affects the character of a listed building, so it may not require listed building consent. In exceptional examples period kitchen fittings, which sometimes survive in twentieth-century listed buildings may come under the listing. In these cases, the period fittings are likely to be protected but in most cases kitchens are a relatively modern addition and should be seen as a disposable feature subject to change over time and fashion.

Can I add on a garden room, conservatory or extension?

Listed building consent and planning permission are regularly granted for garden rooms, conservatories and extensions to listed buildings. However, they are regularly refused too. It would be a mistake to assume that every listed building can be extended but many can, particularly on less significant elevations or in locations where they replace poorly designed extensions that already exist. The key is to get good design advice and avoid proposals that dominate or detract from the character of the listed building itself. Hopefully extensions built today can add to the special

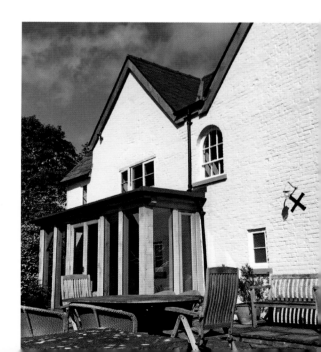

Additions such as this oak-framed garden room are a popular feature of many listed properties, provided the right consents are sought along with an appropriate design.

Listed property dos and don'ts

Do

- Do look for a house that suits your needs. It may sound obvious but if you want a five-bedroom house don't buy a two-bedroom cottage on the basis that you can extend it. The likelihood is that you will not get consent because part of the charm of the cottage is that it is small.
- Do investigate if alterations have been made without consent. Your conveyancing solicitor and surveyor will be able to assist with this but there are checks that you can make too: ask the vendor if they have made alterations; speak to the neighbours; check that the building fits the statutory list description; check the local authority planning register.
- Do establish when the building was listed by referring to the National Heritage List in the relevant nation.
- Do note what attracts you to a particular building. Many listed building owners want to change their building beyond all recognition, not realising that the charm and character that attracted them to the building in the first place is fragile and can be easily lost through relatively small alterations.
- Do get the right professional advice. Surveyors, architects and structural engineers tend to specialise; they are not all experts when it comes to listed buildings. The professional institutions (RIBA, RICS and ICE) all have conservation accreditation schemes so you can identify the right expert and be sure you are getting the right advice.
- Do read up on what makes traditional building construction distinct from modern buildings. Understanding conservation principles or how old buildings need to breathe will help you to engage with your surveyor or your conservation officer. It will also help to inform how you carry out repairs, resolve damp issues or redecorate.
- Do consider joining an organisation like the Listed Property Owners' Club or the Society for the Protection of Ancient Buildings (see page 237).
- Do employ skilled craftspeople to carry out any repairs.

Don't

- Don't be scared of buying a listed building. A little bit of bureaucracy and paperwork is not an unreasonable price to pay for owning a small part of our heritage.
- Don't rely on salespeople, estate agents or contractors to provide reliable advice. If you need guidance it's always best to turn to a professional where you can be certain that advice is not tainted by the desire to sell you their service or product.
- Don't listen to the estate agent who tells you that it is only the outside of the building that is listed. This is a common fallacy and it could get you into trouble as listing protection extends equally to the inside of the building.
- Don't skimp on buildings insurance. Listed buildings can cost more to repair so it is important to get proper advice on the rebuilding cost.
- Don't take the contractor's word for it if they say that listed building consent is not required. It is always worth checking with the local planning authority or a heritage professional.
- Don't treat the conservation officer as the enemy. Ultimately, they want the best thing for the building just like you do and very often they will have a wealth of constructive ideas to help you achieve your aims.
- Don't undervalue historic finishes that speak of generations of owners and craftspeople who created and lived in a house. Once lost the patina of age is impossible to recreate.
- Don't disregard structural or damp problems. They are often not as bad as they first appear but it is important to have them checked out so that they can be remedied.
- Don't be put off by a negative-sounding house buyer's survey. You are paying the surveyor to highlight every possible fault and that is what they will do. In reality, houses are rarely as bad as the report might look at first glance.

character of the listed building and will be cherished by future generations. The most interesting properties are those that have grown and evolved; your plans are just another chapter in its evolution.

Can I put up an outbuilding such as a studio, stables or garage?

All outbuildings, however small, within the curtilage (shadow) of a listed building require planning permission. If they are attached to the building (or a curtilage listed building) they will also require listed building consent. The local planning authority will be interested in the impact the building has on the setting of the listed building and on the amenity of any neighbours.

Listed properties are without doubt one of the most important genres of the nation's housing market. Their historic importance goes way beyond their architectural merits; they are valuable survivors through which we can trace our social and architectural development. If there is any doubt as to their significance, just imagine a world without them, where once beautiful and fascinating buildings had fallen victim to inappropriate change at the hands of those ignorant of the history they contain and describe.

To ignore their value as homes is to walk away from a rich vein of remarkable properties. Accepting the chance to own one does come with an overriding sense of responsibility, but the reward is to revel in the fact that you are helping to look after, and hand on, a significant building that has earned its right to be preserved for future generations. It is often said that as listed building owners we are custodians, guardians that have a duty to care for them during our tenure, a perspective I share with all those I've met that are lucky enough to do just that.

This stunning timber-framed former cartmaker's cottage has seen some dramatic changes to its size and style since it was first built in the fourteenth century.

Listed building owners, Worcestershire

In the summer of 2018, Jonnie Irwin set about helping Nick and Melissa to find a new country home in rural Worcestershire.

Happy customers. Having the chance to meet up with those buyers we've helped find a new rural life is always an inspiring treat.

Having spent the last 22 years living in Surrey raising a family and establishing a successful IT logistics business, they felt the time had come to head more than 100 miles west to the Welsh borders and Worcestershire to be closer to their sons. Armed with a handsome budget of £900,000, they finally bought the first property Jonnie showed them, a stunning Grade II-listed, timber-framed, former cartmaker's cottage that over the years had been much extended, giving them the four bedrooms, landscaped gardens and bags of character they had been looking for. Complete with the bonus of a swimming pool, their new home is within walking distance of the local village with a pub, village hall and historic church.

It was clear from the outset that it was love at first sight for Nick and Melissa but the fact it was listed did not go unnoticed. Like many buyers who've never encountered a listed building before, they had their reservations, not least concerns that they might be held responsible for any changes previous owners might have made without first gaining the right consents. However, following comprehensive legal enquiries by their conveyancing solicitor, their worries were put aside. The focus of the property's listing was the striking timber-framed wing and the stunning inglenook that it contained, which once formed the original kitchen of the old cottage. The historic value of this part of the building was further confirmed with the chance find of a page from a fourteenth-century prayer book that was discovered in the roof space during some remedial work.

Now some nine months into their move they have absolutely no regrets: 'The fact this is listed is no longer of any concern. If it hadn't been it might not have survived as the kind of property we fell in love with. Its imperfections are what make it perfect for us, and while there are changes we would like to make in the future, with the help of our conservation officer we know we can come up with a plan that will allow us to make it ours. What's more, working within the guidelines means we'll do so sympathetically as the current guardians of this very special building that is most definitely our forever home.'

CHAPTER 5

Living with thatch

When most of us try to imagine the perfect rural retreat, there can be little doubt that thatched properties offer a picture of the quintessential country home. For thousands of years, reaching far back into the prehistory of the Neolithic, Bronze and later Iron Ages, the practice of using reed and later straw, as a practical and readily available source of roofing material, is as old as the hills. From the simple round houses of the past, through to Saxon halls, medieval manors and classic cottages, the skills and materials used represent one of the most traditional methods of keeping our homes both warm and dry.

These days of course most houses you are likely to see are roofed with either stone, slate or terracotta tiles. It was the Romans who first introduced terracotta to Britain 2,000 years ago and, as the Welsh will tell you, since the industrialisation of slate quarries at the turn of the nineteenth century, it is Wales that has kept much of Britain – and at the time its growing empire – dry too.

The result is that thatched properties tend only to remain in areas where there has long been a ready source of the materials needed – a pattern that also reflects the geology of the British Isles, and the absence of stone, slate or clay deposits in the regional landscape. East Anglia, the Kent Weald, Wiltshire, the Cotswolds and neighbouring Herefordshire are just some of the areas where you'll find

Thatched cottages like this one on the Welsh borders broker an image of many regard as the ideal rural retreat.

beautiful thatched properties, although, for me, Dorset stands out as one of the prime thatch hotspots.

In a similar way to listed properties, thatched homes can also divide opinion. While many house hunters may love the aesthetics of thatch, many share reasonable concerns about upkeep and safety, not least the fire risks that accompany the other much sought after feature in many country homes, a roaring fire or wood burner.

There is no dodging the fact that as an organic material, thatch does need a high degree of ongoing maintenance and sensible care, and some insurers won't entertain it. That said, there are companies that understand it and offer tailored policies to suit, while around the country an established network of expert thatchers is on hand to provide advice and skills for the property owner. If you do buy a thatched home, the chances are the vendors will be able to give you details of the local thatcher who will know your property well, having worked on it in the past.

How it works

It is often assumed that thatched roofs might be damp, or at risk of letting water in. If left horizontal, a bundle of thatch of whatever material would fail in a heavy rainfall, but the secret long known to the builders and roofers of the past is in the pitch of the roof itself. Put simply, a thatched roof tends to be steeper, ideally 50 degrees, allowing water to run off it quickly, making good use of the pronounced overhang at the eaves. Not surprisingly, most don't require guttering provided the overhang sheds water sufficiently far from the building it protects. This unmistakable roof line often means you can tell if a property currently slated was originally covered in thatch.

Most thatched roofs are in total about 10–15in thick, but it's the upper layer or coat work, the top 6in, that does the work, and of this it's only the top inch that actually gets really wet. Of course, it dries quickly too. It's fixed in place with steel crooks or hazel spars, essentially short lengths twisted

into staples, which tie into the main body of the thatch. It is not uncommon to find with many historic thatched cottages that the underlying material could be as old as the building itself, while the upper layers will have been replaced repeatedly over time. In some rare examples, it's possible to see blackened beams and thatch in the loft space, which reveals the origins of the building as an early hall house, where the smoke from a central hearth would have risen up and out of the apex long before subsequent floors or a bespoke chimney were added.

Materials

It's a common misconception that all thatched properties are covered in the same material. There are essentially three different types of thatching material that reflect the areas from which they are harvested. They all require slightly different approaches to their use, giving each option a unique style that when seen side by side can often allow the keen observer to tell where in the country a property is, and what has been used to roof it.

Longstraw is straw grown specifically for thatching. Modern harvesting techniques and varieties of wheat tend to produce shorter stems, but longstraw is very traditional. It's easily recognised as being more woolly than other types, combining both ends of the wheat stem – the ears and cut butt ends – and will often have more spars showing along the ridge.

Combed wheat is grown as longstraw but the ears and leaf on the stems are removed mechanically giving a slightly crisper appearance. It's particularly common in Dorset, and provides a very definite finish to gable ends and eaves.

Water reed is most commonly seen in East Anglia and localised wetland areas, and is the longest lasting thatch material. The water-repellent properties of water reed speak for themselves, but for obvious reasons it doesn't grow everywhere.

Like a new coat, a re-thatched roof brings a new lease of life to many buildings while also showcasing the crisp finish of a skilled thatcher. In the picture on the left the base layers have been replaced with fire board and an entirely new thatch roof, in contrast to the example below left, which has maintained its original base while enjoying timely repair. The finished article, can be seen below right, as the final touches are made to the ridge. The honey-coloured new straw will soon weather to a characteristic silver-grey.

Ongoing maintenance and costs

The lifespan of a newly thatched roof can be affected by several factors. The quality of materials is one, as is the skill of the thatcher, but the local climate and aspect of the house are also important. North-facing aspects tend to attract more lichen and moss, as well as those that face prevailing weather conditions, while those in shady hollows or surrounded by thick tree cover will also suffer.

Wire mesh is often employed over a roof to limit bird and rodent damage. Important areas to look out for are the flashing around the chimney, and the quality of the ridge that runs along the top of the roof. Ridges usually need attention every 10–15 years depending on materials and aspect, and you'll often see intricate figures such as rabbits, pheasants, foxes or ducks beautifully crafted atop them. Not only can these be great fun, such as the sight of a fox chasing a chicken, they often act as a signature of the enterprising and skilful thatcher who is showing off his craft.

In terms of costs, even back in the 1930s it was estimated that to re-roof a thatched building of average size would match the cost of a family car. Of course, in those days this would equate to a few hundred pounds; yet today this rough rule of thumb persists. Many owners I meet deliberately save a sum every year so that when maintenance is required, funds are already in place, avoiding a shock to the family finances.

Fire risk

The perceived risk of fire and concerns over maintenance has in my experience been the deciding factor for many on whether to buy a thatched property. These days the risks are much better understood thanks to some studies that have looked at thatch fires with the same forensic approach that might govern an air crash investigation.

The latest report by the Fire Protection Agency, commissioned by Historic England in 2014, now recommends that wood burners and multi-fuel stoves should not be fitted to thatched properties because of the intense heat they generate. It's now widely accepted that the main cause of fires is chimney-related due to a build-up of tar through burning of inappropriate fuels; sparks coming out of the flue can deposit hot embers onto a roof, particularly when a fire is being lit and the burner has been over-vented.

In the past, spark guards have been recommended but the report concluded that they had little effect in mitigating the risks, while the height of the chimney and distance of the pot or cowl from the body of the roof did make a difference. Ideally this should be at least 6ft above the roof ridge, but the key thing is to take advice from your thatcher.

Other preventative measures include installing a bird cowl to prevent nest building in the top of the chimney and fitting fire retardant boards to the roof if you can strip all the thatch off and start again. In theory, should a roof ignite, the boards will prevent the fire spreading quickly inside, allowing firefighters time to dowse and pull the thatch off the roof if they are able to. Lining your chimney with a insulated liner is also highly recommended; it will prevent sparks getting out of holes in the chimney breast that might have been caused by failing masonry, and provides invaluable peace of mind.

That said, open fires have of course been a fact of life in our thatched properties for generations. They are a much simpler solution to the problem of keeping warm and are now seen as a safer option when it comes to thatch because they operate in a far calmer way and at lower temperatures, proving once again that when it comes to country life, it's often the old tried and tested traditional ways that are the best, and for good reason.

Every period property of the sort that make the countryside such an architecturally rewarding place requires care and attention. There really is no such thing as the maintenance-free house. I quite understand the reservations many have about thatch, but in truth it is a time-honoured, tested and beautiful material that brings much distinction and historic substance to some of the most beautiful parts of the country.

CHAPTER 6

Running your country home

The basics

When it comes to running your country home, it is not uncommon to find that of the three main utilities of water, sewage and fuel, at least one won't have a mains connection, in contrast to what you might expect in a large village, town or city.

Properties that enjoy a degree of seclusion will often not have any sort of mains provision. Many will have their own source of water in the form of a well or borehole, sewage may go into a septic tank or bio-digester and, in terms of fuel, supplies of either oil or gas may well be stored in your own purpose-installed tank.

The safe and timely provision of these vital services, and their management, is therefore down to you, the home owner, so it's important to understand how these things work. The vendors, neighbours or agents will be able to advise you of the existing arrangements so that you can carry on with the same suppliers if you wish, but either way making sure you are never without the basics of fuel, power and water is today no more challenging than ordering groceries online.

Water, wells and waste

Water is of course the one thing none of us can do without; be it pumped though the mains or up from your own well or borehole, it's an essential resource regardless of where you live. If you are lucky enough to have your own supply, the chances are you'll be drinking and using the finest water around, provided its source has been properly managed. We are also increasingly aware of the value of water. The increasing use of rainwater harvesting to reduce our consumption, allied to many new techniques for reusing the grey water we send down the plughole from our baths and

Wherever you want to live, none of us can go without power and water.

showers can make for a very sustainable addition to any country home.

Private drainage

Not surprisingly, despite the huge advances in sanitary and drainage arrangements in towns and cities during the Victorian period, the countryside is still catching up. When it comes to sewage, if mains are not available there are broadly two main options, neither of which should be of concern, even if you've never dealt with them before.

The first is the *septic tank*. Modern versions are made from plastic but traditionally they comprised a brick-lined underground chamber that remains a common feature of many country properties, particularly larger ones such as farmhouses. Capacity and amount of use will determine the frequency of emptying but there are plenty of firms who are specifically licensed to do this for you and dispose of the waste appropriately. The vendors should be able to pass on the details of their existing service provider. Some properties, such as those in converted farm complexes, may share one tank between them and will all contribute to the cost of emptying it. I've rarely known of one that needs attention more than once a year, but if you are thinking of renovating surrounding buildings into holiday lets that will share the same tank, capacity is an important consideration and it may pay you to invest in installing a larger modern tank or system that can cope with your plans.

The second option, and one which is increasingly popular in new-builds and renovations, is the bio-digester, which aims to be maintenance-free because the waste it handles is broken down across a three-stage anaerobic process that transforms raw sewage into water, which is then slowly released into the soil below ground. Often distinguished by oval green plastic lids at ground level, the bio-digester is the preferred option for many for whom mains connection is impossible. They are also great for adding to a holiday let as a separate waste solution to an existing septic tank.

Heating your home

There are plenty of innovative solutions to providing heat and power to your home these days, but if it lacks thermal efficiency (and leaks hot air) you'll be wasting your time and money. While it is true that many recent renovations will have been undertaken to meet current, or recent, standards of building regulation, most classic rural properties are older and less thermally efficient than new-builds. When evaluating any improvements you might make to the system that heats your home, it is therefore important to understand which one is right for your property and your budget.

Mix it up

I've always favoured a mix of heat sources, including solid fuel such as a wood burner. If something fails there is always the guarantee that you can boil a kettle over a wood stove and keep at least part of your home warm during a cold snap or power cut. I have always lived in houses that have had their own tank to supply oil for central heating, while pressurised tanks containing liquefied petroleum gas (LPG) are now common. Various handy devices are also available to help you monitor how much fuel you have, and a large network of providers exist in rural areas to ensure that topping up your supply is as easy as ordering milk.

Storage

The key factor to consider is the capacity of your tank; put simply, the bigger the better. The more you can buy at once, the cheaper it will be per unit of fuel, and in many communities, syndicates exist that allow several households to order fuel at the same time, ensuring an economy of scale that could reduce your bill by several pence per litre. Larger tanks also allow you to buy in the summer and autumn when prices are naturally lower, enabling you to get through the winter without concern, depending on the size of your home and rates of consumption.

Biomass boilers

Boilers that use wood pellets or wood chip are an increasingly popular option. They can be expensive to purchase and install but the fuel for biomass boilers is generally significantly cheaper than more conventional fuels. You will also benefit from renewable heat incentive payments, which will offset the cost of buying and running your boiler. Biomass units do require a reasonably large space for installation, storage for your fuel and good access for the delivery of the pellets or chip. I've seen several examples in operation. Note that you will need to be vigilant to make sure it continues to operate smoothly, but they can be a very good option for rural properties.

The good news is that innovation in this area is continuing apace so keep an eye out for news of more options for domestic boilers that are fuelled with a wider range of materials, including household waste.

Air source and ground source heat pumps

Air source heat pumps transfer heat absorbed from the outside air into an indoor space via a fan-based system to provide heating, or a conventional central heating system to provide both heat and hot water. They can also act as a cooling system in the summer months.

These systems have a low carbon footprint, and can be powered by wind energy or solar power rather than electricity. They can also attract payments through the UK's renewable heat incentive as well as reducing your ongoing utility costs. They have the added advantage too of not requiring any space for fuel storage.

You should be aware however that the heat supply will be lower than with conventional oil or gas boilers so you may need larger radiators. Underfloor or warm-air heating may be a better option. One possible disadvantage of these systems is that they can be noisy when running, in a similar way to air-conditioning units.

Ground source heat pumps work on the same principle of heat transfer, in this case taking heat from the ground to the inside of your house, or vice versa for cooling. Installation of ground source pumps is complex, relying either on a bore hole (330ft deep) or loops of pipework buried at least 5ft underground, which can be expensive, but they have the advantage of very low operating costs, use no fuels and don't produce any carbon emissions.

Power

I still know a handful of hardy souls who live a life beholden to an old generator run on diesel in the wildest corners of the UK, but let's face it, it's not for everyone. However, going green can be expensive, as is the task of getting power direct from the grid to farms and barns with no power that are up for conversion. If you are thinking of taking on a property or project that requires electricity, but has no existing supply, be wary of how much it may cost at the outset.

Renewables

These days there are many tried and tested renewable sources that have been developed for the domestic market and which lend themselves to rural life, particularly in more isolated locations.

Damaged or blocked gutters can have serious consequences for your home, while an immediate fix could save you a fortune later on.

Solar energy is derived from the sun's radiation harnessed through panels. Technology is improving all the time, and options for storing the energy generated in solar battery storage systems are increasing its versatility. This is a genuinely renewable energy source that will never run out and will save you money through reduced bills and payments for any surplus that can be sold back to the grid.

Solar technology can be utilised as a direct source of electric power (photovoltaic or PV) and as a supplement to hot water and central heating systems (solar thermal). More recently it has been possible to combine both in PVT. As well as reducing your energy bills, you can enjoy low maintenance costs with a solar system; giving your panels a good clean a couple of times a year being the main requirement.

Like air and ground sourced energy, the initial investment in installation can be high. You will also need to consider the impact of the British climate on your solar system: cloudy and rainy days will obviously reduce its efficiency. Nor will it

Getting connected

In September 2018, retired policeman Martin moved into a secluded cottage in the Shropshire hills. With stunning views and nothing but the sound of the local wildlife, he was set fair for a life that was light years away from his old home in Hatfield. Yet despite relishing the chance to enjoy a more remote life, he didn't want to be completely isolated, but the house he was buying had no internet connectivity and no terrestrial or satellite television signal. The answer was satellite broadband. His local provider was able to relay a signal from a farmhouse across the valley within line of sight. Because his landline was not capable of delivering a speed greater than 2Mb/s, the government paid for installing the satellite receiver, now discretely mounted on his cottage. He now gets 30Mb/s, while also hosting a further receiver, which relays to a neighbour in the other direction.

work at night so planning is required to get the best out of it.

With any of these options, you will need to consider whether your home is listed or sits within a conservation area, as permissions will be needed.

Open fires and wood burners

One of the most attractive and sought-after features in any country home is a working fireplace, be it a cavernous inglenook or cosy wood burner, but there are some important things you should bear in mind.

For the purists, a roaring fire in an iron basket or braced on ancient firedogs is the ultimate focal point, and little can beat the sweet smell of well-seasoned wood smoke, but wood burners can also cast a spell over many period homes and are increasingly being incorporated into new-build or contemporary conversions too. Tending to a fire clearly taps into something ancient and visceral within us all.

Wood burners

- The advantages of the wood burner are many. Because the business of combustion is contained within a cast-iron stove, the careful management of airflow means that much higher temperatures can be reached. The result is a fire that burns more efficiently, while the heat radiates through the burner itself and isn't simply sent up the chimney.
- Open fires typically lose 75 per cent of their heat up the flue, whereas most modern wood burners work the other way around, pumping 75 per cent of their heat back into your room. To put their value in context, it's reckoned that an open fire would consume 16 logs in generating 5Kw of heat, whereas a modern wood burner would need just 5kW, a figure well worth considering when thinking about running costs.
- Do consider installing a wood burner approved by Defra or a clean-burning, Ecodesign Ready model. Local authorities

To enjoy a lazy afternoon or evening bathed in the dry heat and gentle crackle of an open fire is to share in the fellowship of all those who have done exactly that over many centuries in the same place, providing a direct and emotive connection to the past.

Contemporary wood burners feel right at home in any setting, but this one more than complements this stunning, green oak new-build by Border Oak.

are unlikely to impose limitations on the use of fires and stoves outside urban areas, but it is important to be mindful of the environmental impact of their use.

- Wood burners also have the advantage of being much safer to use; containing the heat also holds in the sparks and reduces the fire risk, meaning you can shut the doors on a roaring fire without worrying, although care should be taken when installing in thatched properties (page 51).

Fuel

Using 'clean' fuel is very important. The main problem regarding pollution from open fires and wood burners occurs when burning wet or unseasoned wood. Always seek seasoned hardwood such as oak, ash and beech, as opposed to softwoods like spruce or pine. Put simply, seasoned wood has been given time to dry, but it does require patience. If you can harvest wood of your own, it's worth remembering that you should leave it to dry for at least a couple of summers, around 18 months depending on the species, and somewhere out of the rain with good airflow around it.

In contrast, dry softwood makes excellent kindling to start your fire, such as finely chopped old pallet wood or builders' off-cuts, and it's much cheaper than buying bundles of kindling that you'll find in garages and some supermarkets.

Burning the right fuel will greatly affect the lifespan and efficiency of your burner. If you go down the multi-fuel route and are thinking of coal or anthracite, follow the manufacturer's guidelines on exactly which type of solid fuel to use. I've heard many tales of the wrong fuel being used that, within the efficient confines of a cast-iron stove, has burnt too hot and become out of control. Likewise, some areas now only permit smokeless fuel, so do check.

CHOOSING YOUR WOOD BURNER

There are five main factors to consider when choosing to install or replace a wood burner in your home.

1 Safety Many older country properties may have had a chimney flue blocked up at the point where it enters the room, while others may have had the chimney itself removed from the roof and the hole tiled or slated over. Always check that there is a working flue and, if not, the safest solution is to install a flexible liner that will sit within the existing chimney and connect to your burner or open fire. If in any doubt seek the advice of a reputable sales outlet and installer (see page 237).

Also make sure you have fitted a bird cowl to the chimney pot. This simple metal mesh will prevent birds nesting in your chimney, particularly through the warmer months when your fire may be infrequently used. Nests can be a cause of chimney fires and should always be checked for if you are buying a property that may have been empty for a while.

You should also sweep your working flues and chimneys at least once a year, and always in a property that's new to you. Never assume it's been done. If swept regularly you will remove the build-up of tar and ash that, if left unchecked, could lead to a chimney fire over time.

2 Size Wood burners come in a huge range of shapes, sizes and styles, but before you get carried away with the aesthetics you'll need to work out how big a burner you need. Size is measured in heat output (kW). The accepted formula is based on the dimensions of the room it's going to heat: width × length × height ÷ 14 = kW required.

I would always advise going one higher than the equation suggests. Calculations of exact room size, given the quirks of many old houses, are rarely entirely accurate, and it's better to be too warm than too cold.

3 Looks and legislation The market is packed with a huge range of different styles, but from 2022 all new stoves will have to conform to new Ecodesign legislation. This requires at least 75 per cent efficiency and particle emissions of less than 40mg/m³. If you are about to buy one, check it has the latest SIA Ecodesign Ready label.

We use our wood stove not just for cooking; it's also a fantastic focal point and an essential source of heat.

4 Fuel If you live in a smoke controlled area then burners that can burn smokeless fuel will determine the range you can pick from, otherwise you can choose either wood burning or multi-fuel (wood and coal), which are by far the most common. If you are starting from scratch it's also worth considering a burner, which, if equipped with a back boiler, could contribute to your hot water supply and save money in the long run.

5 Costs In general, you get what you pay for. Beware mild steel versions or cheap imports made of inferior cast iron over those from established manufacturers. As well as numerous British suppliers, it is perhaps no surprise that some of the best come from Scandinavia where the wood burner can be a necessity through the winter and not just a favoured accessory. You will need to plan for the costs of installation too, and this will largely depend on the flue and whether you need to install or replace one. This cost is of course dependent on the flue's height and diameter, typically either 5 or 6in. If affordable, once lit and gracing your home with warmth and light, you'll never want to leave your wood burner's side. It will also help the sale of your home in the future, but be sure to retain your installation certificates for both potential buyers and insurers.

If in doubt, seek a HETAS-approved installer who will take care of the whole process for you, and who can issue a HETAS installation certificate, itself often a prerequisite for insurers and holiday lets and a real help if selling your home on later.

Unseasoned, freshly felled timber will have a moisture content of well over 60 per cent, so it's essential to store and season it in dry conditions for at least 12–18 months to a point where that figure will reduce, ideally to 15 per cent. Attempting to burn unseasoned wood could, over time, clog your flue with flammable residues. Seasoned wood will also give you a hotter, safer fire. Moisture meters are an invaluable tool for checking whether your wood supply is ready to go.

Maintaining your country home

It is a fact that most properties you are likely to view if you are in search of a classic Escape to the Country home will be historic to some degree. It follows therefore that, like an old car, they will need regular maintenance. The easiest way to organise the care of your new (old!) home is to work very simply from the top to the bottom.

Next to fire, the most damaging element for a property is water. Once it gets in it will rapidly accelerate decay and damp, encourage the activity of wood-boring insects, and cause a significant hazard if it encounters your electricity supply.

Damp is often described as rising damp, and dozens of suppliers and products will claim to be able to eradicate or block it, but in reality, few seem to work. The way to tackle damp, wherever you find it, is to trace and address the source of the water that is causing it.

Your roof is the first place to start when ensuring that your home is water-tight; check for missing or broken tiles and then check the flashings (the lead work that surrounds openings for chimneys and skylights or dormer windows, and forms gullies in the roof). It's also important to check your rainwater goods; your gutters and drainpipes, which can easily become blocked and cause water to cascade down walls. A good time to do this is after the autumn leaf fall.

You should also check your walls. If your house is brick built, then look out for spalling – the degradation of the face of bricks, or failing pointing. If your house is rendered, look for cracks or bulges where the render may have come away from the wall behind it. If left unchecked, these issues can prove much more expensive in the long run so timely repair is critical.

Many rural properties do not have the damp course that is standard in modern builds. Modern houses will usually have a strip of polythene a few courses of bricks up, which will serve to stop damp travelling up the wall from the ground. My old cottage had a damp course made from roofing slate,

standard practice in early nineteenth-century Wales. The cottage had almost no foundations either, not an approach that we'd take today, but the fact that the cottage is still standing 200 years later is a tribute to those early building methods.

A common cause of damp is an external ground level that's higher than the internal floor or damp course, often seen in houses built on sloping ground or hillsides. This is known as 'bridging' and the best solution is to lower the ground level to enable the damp course to work as it should. Another option is to install a French drain (a trench filled with gravel or rock or containing a perforated pipe), which should take the water safely away to prevent moisture 'rising'.

Climbing plants can also cause problems. While they look attractive, bear in mind the impact they may have on your home. Ivy, for example, can penetrate mortar joints between bricks or stone causing damage and allowing water in.

Breathability

Modern houses tend to be built with cavity walls (formed from two walls of bricks or blocks with a gap between them) but this has not always been the case. Up until the early part of the twentieth century, most houses were built with solid

Areas of high rainfall, such as in Cumbria seen below, can be unforgiving on buildings, especially those built into hillsides and slopes.

walls using materials that could 'breathe' – that is water could pass a small distance through the external face of the brickwork when it rained, but would evaporate back out in the sun or wind. Similarly, moisture generated inside the house caused by cooking or washing could pass in and out of the lime plaster-covered walls, and be dried out by the heat from fires and airflow through the house.

Throughout the latter part of the twentieth century many alterations were made to houses that have impaired their ability to breathe. Misguidedly intended to address damp issues (rather than dealing with the cause of the damp), 'solutions' such as cement rendering walls, applying 'plastic' paints or waterproofing treatments will have added to the problems over time. This is an issue we are facing in our own house and we are slowly removing such materials and replacing them with breathable alternatives to protect the integrity of our timber-framed home for the long term.

Porth Farm House near Towan Beach in Cornwall shows off its natural stone fabric, mercifully unfettered with modern render which could otherwise cause great damage.

The four main causes of damp

1 Penetrating damp water getting from the outside to the inside, caused by building defects such as those outlined above, and the most common cause of damp. It is usually localised and causes damage to internal finishes. The solution is to rectify the problem that is allowing the water into the building.

2 Condensation usually characterised by black spots of mould on the walls and caused by high levels of moisture in the air condensing on cold surfaces. Damp caused by condensation is often found in bathrooms or behind cupboards on external walls where there is insufficient airflow. This can usually be resolved by improving ventilation.

3 Rising damp caused by external ground levels being higher than internal floor levels and resolved by lowering the ground level and improving drainage. A drain inspection is a good investment as cracked or broken drains can lead to further problems over time.

4 Plumbing leaks leaking pipes, toilet soil pipes or shower trays can cause significant damage to old houses if left unchecked. A significant failure will be easy to identify, but slow drips or leaks can be harder to spot. Dry rot, or fungal decay of timber, is a high risk in conditions such as these and can be difficult and expensive to resolve. As ever, the key is to find the source of the dampness and address it straight away.

CHAPTER 7

Rural businesses and holiday lets

For many of the buyers that we meet on the show, their move to the country has been prompted by retirement, but with ever more flexible working arrangements, your escape doesn't need to wait until then. A move to the country may also be a good opportunity to explore a change in your professional life by setting up a business of your own.

The route towards making ends meet through holiday lets or glamping sites is well worn, but I'm increasingly meeting adventurous souls who are keen to develop their artisan skills into viable businesses. Working from home is a huge attraction, supported by the steady roll-out of super-fast broadband to rural areas. Nonetheless starting any business from scratch is a huge challenge, and while the online world and the explosion of home delivery networks is making a sizeable contribution to the rural business framework, help is at hand in the form of a recently established, nationwide initiative: the Rural Business Awards.

Back in late 2014 entrepreneurs Jemma Clifford and Anna Price (pictured right) decided the time had come to champion the increasing success of rural businesses. Each of them very aware of the many unique challenges faced by rural businessmen and women, their concerns soon gave rise to the foundation of an organisation that aims to help. The RBAs have now established a forum that seeks to highlight the best of rural business initiatives across the UK. From modest table-top artisan craftsmen and women, to farmers and producers who've diversified, and a huge range of IT and financial services to leisure, tourism, education and real estate interests, their initiative has now developed into the Rural Business Group. Designed to help both existing and first-time rural entrepreneurs, it aims to connect them with experts who can help new ideas and products succeed.

How to turn your business dreams into reality

1 Do your research

Before starting a business, you need to understand your market and its potential – there's no point in coming up with an amazing innovative product if, in fact, no one wants to buy it.

Ask yourself: where your idea fits within the marketplace; what purpose it serves; and whether it solves a problem or takes away someone's business headache. A strategic plan and a clear vision of your product or service are essential, no business will survive without them.

2 Read and learn and question

Starting a business is a real learning curve, so start early and absorb as much information as you can. Try to ask questions of people with experience, or those who understand your market and your customers.

3 Consider risk and what it looks like to you

Setting up any business comes with risks. Before you launch yourself into the process, take a moment to identify and address some of the reasons you think you shouldn't or can't start a business. By getting these out of your head now, they won't hold you back in the future.

4 Celebrate/inhabit/accept your niche

As far as possible, keep things simple. Don't try to be all things to all people – you don't need to. Your business will naturally evolve and develop its offering as it grows, but as a start-up you need to have laser focus on a core 'solution' to deliver.

5 Know your numbers

At the very least it's imperative to develop a comprehensive forecast – projecting income and expenditure. As business founders, you cannot be an expert in everything, but finance is an area you shouldn't take risks in.

6 Network

It's important to find your tribe – to connect with like-minded people, and other businesses facing similar challenges. Successful networking is founded on reciprocity: give as much as you take, engage with people who value the same things as you do and get stuck in – you get out what you put in!

7 Be brave

Oh yes. Never ever doubt that running your own business requires bravery – some might say you need to be a little crazy. But if you believe in your dream and can articulate your passion you are halfway there.

8 Understand your regional and local business support structure

Before you run into any problems, find out where you can go for advice. Quite often business advice is free if you know where to look – a good networking group should help to signpost resources that are available.

Business support and funding advice provided by Local Enterprise Partnerships (LEPs) and Growth Hubs can be invaluable, if a little city-centric. However, having links to city-based businesses is no bad thing where specific business advice is concerned.

9 Hold your horses!

Don't be sold services without understanding exactly what it is you need – always ask yourself do I really *need* this or is it simply something they are looking to sell?

By 'doing your research' (point 1) you put yourself firmly in the driving seat – let your strategy guide you *and* your service providers. It's *your* business – maintain control.

10 Be authentic and remember your WHY

Most importantly, don't lose sight of the reason why you are setting up your business, or pretend to be something or someone you are not. It will catch up with you in the end. Plus, people warm to authenticity.

Holiday lets

Few factors influence a house search as much as the wish to buy a property with the potential to generate its own income. Prime among them is the idea that a holiday let will allow you to fund your new life by providing holiday accommodation for hordes of visitors who, like you, yearn to spend time in your chosen location.

To some extent it's a dream well worth pursuing, but take care not to lose sight of the fact that you should aim to bring something to the holiday market that is memorable and a treat, a unique experience for your guests that will leave them not only wanting to return, but also prepared to recommend it to others. Holiday letting is not a new idea, and a saturated market in some areas means that competition can be high, with the result that only the best are busy and lucrative.

Holiday lets can be very successful contributors to household income, and useful overspill space for visiting family and friends, but relying on them as a main source of income can bring some risks. That said, there are a great many that can turn over a significant amount if done to the highest standards in the right area.

If you've ever made use of one of the thousands of very tempting lets available the length and breadth of the country, you'll know what's required. Ideally it should offer something that the holidaymaker may not have the chance to experience at home. Views are a good starting point, but at the very least it should offer a real escape from the hustle and bustle of everyday life. Holiday lets that immerse your visitors in a quintessential vision of country life are bound to be the most successful. Good quality furnishings and fittings, sumptuous textiles and, of course, a wood burner or open fire all score highly in the list of holiday let must-haves, but it also needs to be practical to run and maintain. One of your most important considerations will be the ease of turning your holiday let round in the few hours between bookings. For many buyers, it is the hands-on running of a holiday let

business that they seek, but it is perfectly possible to subcontract out the day-to-day chores. If you broker your let through an agent, the better ones will also offer a turnaround and maintenance service, leaving you, the owner, with little to do. Services like these can add significantly to your cost however, and will reduce your profits accordingly.

It is also worth considering your market. Are you going for couples, families with young children and/or those with dogs? Ideally all should be capable of welcoming those with disabilities and I've seen many beautiful holiday homes with well thought-out and accessible facilities. Likewise, those that cater for well-behaved dogs also do very well, but you've got to consider the impact on cleaning and weekly turnaround time.

With many properties available to book online, you can sneak a peek at their digital calendars to get an idea of how busy they are at different times of year, as well as a useful steer on the standards required to charge good rates. I've always felt that if you can offer a five-star product at four-star prices you won't go far wrong. Doing your homework and testing different price points and occupancy levels in a simple spreadsheet will provide a useful guide as to how much you might turn over.

Of course, the more lets you have the better the chance of creating a business that will sustain you, or at least one that will make a determined contribution to your annual income. This is important when considering converting an outbuilding into lets, once you've got the requisite planning permission. As a rule of thumb, I'd always suggest creating a let with reasonable space rather than trying to squeeze in a greater number. Ask yourself the simple question: would what you're designing please you once you've got out of the car on a dark and wet Friday night after a long drive?

You should also consider how intrusive it's likely to be to you. In my experience buyers with high budgets often come down to earth with a bump when they realise just how close their guests will be to their own everyday family life. For some, the chance to meet new friends is a bonus and all part of the lifestyle they are seeking to create, while others still want a sense of peace and quiet as their new business earns its keep. The flipside of course is that most holidaymakers don't want to feel that they are intruding into the owners' space any more than they want their week away to be overlooked. At the end of the day my guess is that most of us go to the countryside for a relaxing break unfettered with nosy neighbours, be they fellow holidaymakers or landlords.

Location and views are everything when it comes to glamping, regardless of the offering. The wigwam (above) has character and position, whereas the cabin (top) offers an all-year-round option. However the simple yurt, left, has often been transformed by glampers into an exotic, spacious and memorable escape.

I've long been a huge fan of shepherd's huts because they are easily moved. This example (opposite and above left) by Riverside Shepherd Huts is an en-suite, year-round option that is ready to earn its keep as soon as it arrives. An equally popular, although more permanent alternative are glamping pods, (below left and above) such as these at Wigwam Holidays near Builth Wells in Wales.

Financial considerations

In addition to planning how your holiday let is managed and presented there are some important financial considerations too.

There are special mortgage considerations for holiday lets that differ from those for residential and buy-to-let mortgages such as minimum income requirements; a deposit of 25–30 per cent as a minimum; and rental income expectations (that could be 150 per cent of the mortgage cost, for example). Agents' experience will be invaluable in projecting realistic rental income expectations.

You will also need to take some advice on the tax implications of running a holiday let business, to make sure that you are benefiting from any relevant tax relief such as capital allowances, and claiming all allowable expenses (such as repairs, mortgage interest, cleaning, letting commission, utilities etc.), but also so you are aware of potential liabilities such as capital gains tax. Keep an eye on your total gross rental income too as you may need to register for value added tax (VAT).

Your local council will charge business rates on your holiday let (as it's a business), but you may qualify for small business rate relief.

Money-saving tips

• Equipping a holiday let from scratch can be expensive. Consider goods and fittings that can be easily maintained or replaced but which also combine comfort and style with practicality of cleaning. Excessive clutter is no substitute for inspiring interior design. If you'd live with it, so will your guests!

• One low-budget way to decorate your holiday let is to furnish it with inspiring pictures of the local area that you have taken and framed with inexpensive frames. You can also order bespoke wallpaper that's a map of the region, which can add immediate impact and interest to hallways.

• Another cheap way to add value to your guests' stay is to provide a comprehensive, up-to-date file containing details of local attractions, walks and places to eat and drink; people are always thrilled to hear about hidden gems.

• If you are buying an existing business, you may find that you can buy many of the contents, particularly if the vendor is downsizing, giving you the option of keeping the let open with current bookings. You can then tweak the aesthetics later.

Rooms and properties with a view are always popular, not least those near the sea (opposite below), as are those that also offer a wood burner (opposite above). While the promise of a cosy stay in a picturesque thatch can be a draw in itself regardless of location (below).

A landlord's tale

First-time buyers of a holiday let.

In 2010 Nicola and Luke set about finding a suitable property to buy and let close to their existing new home in Herefordshire. Pool Head Cottage is now an established and busy holiday let set in beautiful countryside near Westhide to the north of Hereford, which affords its guests access to huge swathes of this popular part of the Welsh Borders.

For Nicola this was a step into the unknown. What to buy, what to offer and how much to charge to establish a business that would repay the investment were crucial and challenging questions. As with many entering the holiday let market for the first time, key to success was creating and crafting a product that would quickly be financially viable and self-sustaining. Issues such as should

they market the property via an agent, and how they would manage the turnarounds and maintenance, were essential questions that all needed answers. After much trial and effort Nicola's keen to share the lessons they've learned.

1 Identify your market It is important to consider why people would come to your property for a holiday. Is your property near a popular tourist attraction or a well-known holiday destination such as a National Park or coastal town? In these cases potential guests will be searching for properties in your specific area.

The high standards offered at Pool Head Cottage in Herefordshire have proved successful in establishing it as a destination in its own right.

If your area is less well known as a holiday destination you need to consider how to make it appeal to guests unfamiliar with the area. We did this by choosing a classic rural property with chocolate box appeal: the house itself is the reason for booking. It is worth investing in professional photographs for your marketing.

2 How to market your property/to use an agent or not Initially we baulked at the cost of using an agent but given that Herefordshire is lesser known as a tourist area we decided that the right agency would have a better reach in terms of marketing nationwide. Essentially, we felt that it was better to earn 80 per cent of the income from 70 per cent occupancy than 100 per cent of the income from a lesser occupancy. It has proved invaluable in attracting visitors looking for a rural getaway regardless of location.

Using an agent has relieved us of the responsibility of managing the bookings, deposits and, on rare occasions, dealing with complaints both from guests and on our behalf after damage left by guests.

As an agent will want to determine the price per night, do take into consideration all your running costs (insurance, utilities, tax etc.) and the turnaround costs (cleaning, laundry, amenities, welcome hamper etc.) when setting a minimum night stay.

After initially having a two-night minimum we realised that the income from two nights barely covered the turnaround costs but we did however find that many guests booking for a short stay returned for longer bookings. Now we have a three-night minimum to cater for long weekends and midweek stays (which I have found have increased and are a valuable source of income in low season) and a five-night minimum at peak times.

If you do decide to use an agency look for one that represents the standards you want to sell at and therefore the income you hope to achieve. Look at the other properties on their site and then try to improve on them as they are your competition! If you are in a popular tourist region and decide to use an agent you can use an area-specific site: if not, opt for a wider-reaching agency that market on a more national basis.

3 Repeat business Returning customers are your goal as a holiday let; it helps build your occupancy levels over time. That, the various review websites and the increasing competition, mean that you must be the best you can be. Your guests' comfort is paramount but there are easy ways to achieve this:
- Make sure the property is warm on arrival and a light is on if it is winter.
- Make the experience as easy as possible; a key safe allows for flexible arrival and departure.
- Guests benefit from being able to control the heating.
- Leave the fire set with plenty of wood.
- Have good quality, neutral furniture and fittings, without clutter, plenty of comfortable seating, storage and pegs for coats/wellies.
- Stock the kitchen with plenty of cooking appliances, tableware, glasses, mugs etc., but also basics such as salt and pepper and teabags.
- Supply the best quality towels and bed linen you can afford, remembering that how they iron is important.
- Provide cleaning equipment for guests to keep the property clean during their stay, from dishwasher tablets to a mop and bucket.
- The finishing touches make all the difference – even down to luxury loo paper.
- A hamper that includes as much local produce as possible makes a lovely welcome.

The agency that we let with were very helpful in providing us with a comprehensive list of things to include in the cottage, advice on furnishings and the use of their trade accounts for purchasing furniture and linens.

(Pool Head Cottage is available to let through Rural Retreats, see page 237.)

CHAPTER 8

The good life

Water, as seen at this riverside property in Derbyshire, attracts many rural settlers.

When thinking about escaping to the country, those of us of a certain age may take some inspiration from the classic 1970s sitcom *The Good Life*. The show pitched the then eccentric environmental ambitions of Tom and Barbara against the entrenched social norms of the day, in the heart of the commuter belt, and it remains a great benchmark for a generation of us wanting to escape the urban rat race.

Yet for all that, very few of the couples I've met on *Escape to the Country* are serious Good Lifers. The majority are happy simply to live in the countryside and enjoy all that it offers. On the other hand, only a very few genuinely seek a life off-grid and aim for a sustainable life of self-sufficiency, for good reason. It takes a huge amount of determination and focus, with a cartload of practical skills and initiative, underpinned by a passion for a lifestyle that can be all-consuming.

I've always had huge respect for those willing and able to achieve self-sufficiency. Spending my late teens and twenties in the Cambrian Mountains, I met many who had managed to do so, lured to the area as refugees of the 1960s and 1970s, a fascinating and eclectic bunch of musicians, writers, artists, retired architects, artisans and even a monk, who found the space, solitude and pace of life they craved in the worn, ancient uplands of Mid Wales. Often supported by little more than an old diesel generator and a refreshing philosophy that *less* really was *more*.

Welsh ecovillage: Lammas

Living off-grid is a worthy ambition, but ensuring that your life is truly sustainable is a huge challenge. It's an ambition that is often at odds with the demands of modern life. Yet in the hills of West Wales, that is exactly what a pioneering bunch of eco-home builders have spent the last 10 years trying to do.

Lammas was set up in 2009 to demonstrate that sustainable Low Impact Design (LID) was possible in the twenty-first century. With the backing of the Welsh Government and the creation of a planning framework titled 'One Planet Development' dedicated to initiatives like Lammas, the project finally got the go-ahead to transform around 80 acres of degraded sheep pasture, providing an initial nine 7.5-acre plots open to anyone willing to develop them within the strict parameters that govern life at this unique undertaking.

Residents are expected to generate 50 per cent of their living costs including food, fuel and income from their plots within five years, while construction of their dwellings must be from locally sourced and sustainable, or recycled, materials. Many who live at Lammas work in local businesses or the service industries while enjoying the very distinct lifestyle that an ecovillage brings. Lammas comes complete with a green,

millpond and community hub, a stunning building built by volunteers that set the project in motion. Funded by the Department for Energy and Climate Change (DECC) the centre also boasts a collection of renewable power sources including solar and hydro, which has ensured the hub itself is entirely off-grid. Residents are encouraged to volunteer on community projects and help their neighbours. Many who have come here had no previous construction experience but it has not held them back.

Hoppi Wimbush was one of its founders and showed me around.

Essentially a collection of smallholdings, Lammas is founded upon the principle that they all work together to create a culture of land-based self-reliance. In so doing Hoppi explained that they have transformed the ecology of their 80-acre site 'from degraded pasture to one full of vitality and abundance'.

The results a decade on have been remarkable. The houses built from locally sourced materials might have graced the set of *The Lord of the Rings*; using tree trunks, stripped branches, straw bales, turf and any number of reclaimed items, their builders and owners have created truly unique structures that both look and feel such a part of their environment they might have sprung from it. At around £20,000–30,000 to build, not only are they the most original and imaginative country properties I have ever seen, they have also proven that good sustainable development is achievable while striving for the highest ecological goals.

A guiding principle behind Lammas is its commitment to share their achievements and inspire others. For visitor opening times and more information visit their website.

Buildings such as the one seen here have been created for as little as £25,000, their design based upon the materials available, many of which have been upcycled.

Smallholdings

Perhaps the easiest route into self-sufficiency is to buy an existing smallholding. The principle behind this is that if you are thinking of having livestock, an existing smallholding should have a ready supply of fenced land, water and shelter, but importantly should also come with a holding number. County Parish Holding (CPH) numbers (both temporary and permanent) are required by law if you intend to keep or move any form of livestock whether for commercial purposes or as pets. CPH numbers are administered by the Rural Payments Agency and are unique to your property. They allow for the safe tracking of livestock around the country, critical given the tragedies of BSE, foot and mouth, and the continued threat from TB.

You can, of course, set about creating your own Good Life anywhere you like, and even if the home you fall in love with doesn't have an existing holding number you can apply for one. Livestock isn't for everybody, but land on which to grow fruit and vegetables often is. This can be achieved with little more than a bit of hard work and a supply of water.

Your animals and other family

If you are keen on keeping livestock, and can comply with any required regulations, you will find the effort hugely rewarding. From keeping a few hens and enjoying fresh eggs, to rearing a much wider range of livestock, the scope is very broad. For the uninitiated, there are plenty of good courses around that will help you on your smallholding journey, and with one-day courses costing around £100, I would highly recommend such an investment before you commit.

While every species and breed has its own issues and challenges, there are some things common to keeping all larger animals that it's worth considering before you commit a sizeable proportion of your budget to buying land upon which to develop your ideas. For more than three generations, my old friend Gareth Wyn Jones's family have farmed the harsh uplands of Snowdonia in the Carneddau

Mountains above Conwy in North Wales. Gareth's irrepressible passion for farming and all that it means has made him an increasingly popular broadcaster and a respected voice for the farming community in Wales and the wider world. It made sense then to ask him to share his thoughts on what to look out for when considering taking on livestock for the first time:

1 Get some experience If you really have never worked with any form of livestock before, see if you can volunteer for a neighbouring farmer; chances are it will be the most useful period in your new life. Owning livestock and taking up farming can to some be a romantic idea, but it's a business that is tough both physically, financially and not least emotionally. They'll show you round the practicalities and introduce you to the realities of life and death on a farm. Producing food has its costs, and there is rarely time to be sentimental.

Another option is to approach World Wide Opportunities on Organic Farms (WWOOF), which offer contacts with gardens, farms and smallholdings where you can get free board and lodging in exchange for help on their land, giving you some valuable experience on the process.

2 Selecting the breed you want It is important to select stock that is well suited to the landscape in which you are going to keep it. Animals need to be hardy and used to the local conditions. If in doubt, ask around the local farming community for help and advice as to what breeds do well in the area. For example, putting a lowland breed of sheep such as Suffolks onto the highlands would be a mistake, but you might succeed in taking an upland breed such as Herdwicks to lower levels. Animals are sensitive to different types of pasture and it's important to understand what your land can sustain, and whether it's been fertilised historically or managed organically.

3 Stock management Once you have selected which animals you want to keep, you should ask your vet for advice and create a plan to enable you to keep them healthy: matters such as injections, mating and gestation times, and land required per head will help you prepare.

4 Holding numbers Your CPH number will lead you to a flock or herd number, which is cross-referenced with the BCMS (British Cattle Movement Scheme). This is essential if you are to buy, sell or move livestock and is the same for every livestock owner. Tags and numbers for specific animals are now stricter than ever after the tragedies of BSE and foot and mouth, ensuring accurate and timely traceability of animals all over the UK and those coming into the country.

5 Breeding stock This subject is a roller-coaster of ups and downs. You must expect good years, poor years, and be prepared to deal with the effects of poor weather, rising costs of supplies and the unpredictable survival rates of animals, all of which can take their toll on your ability to stick with it if you've never experienced it before. There is no shame in trying and then walking away, but all the more reason to do your homework before you start.

6 Don't underestimate the challenge Running a smallholding is hard work. Consider how much time you will have to manage it, when set against your existing commitments. Be realistic! Start small and build up as your knowledge and experience grows; keeping a few chickens (see page 78) is a good place to start.

Gareth sums it up: 'Livestock farmers are a good bunch who are always willing to help. Remember you are going into it for the long term and there is no better feeling than seeing your first lamb born knowing you've bred it. As hunter-gatherers-cum-farmers it's a proud place to be. Farming isn't the preserve of farmers; the more people come into it and

Agricultural ties

Perhaps one of the most curious features of the rural property market is what is known as an Agricultural Tie, or user restriction. The purpose of attaching a tie to a house has been to limit the occupancy to those with a specific occupation, usually related to agriculture or forestry work, and in some exceptional circumstances equestrian trades. Since first introduced as part of the 1948 Town and Country Planning Act, such ties have tended to reduce the value of properties because of the restrictions on who could live in it, but if you can prove it is no longer necessary they can, in some cases, be lifted by the council.

Properties with ties tend to be small because they were built for farmworkers, and while some do come with some land, often woodland, the majority do not. One thing most have in common is that they are sited in some very pretty locations.

VEGETABLE PLOTS

Historically, most rural properties would have allowed space to produce a basic range of vegetables. At the extreme end of the spectrum the nation's great country estates were furnished with huge walled kitchen gardens covering several acres that could supply the finest fruit and vegetables all year round, but the same principles also applied to modest cottages and farms with simple plots. These days the aspiration to enjoy a degree of self-sufficiency from a well-tended veg patch is common to many, but knowing where to start in creating a viable growing area can be a challenge if you are setting about it for the first time, or buying a home that has no established plot.

Since 2003, Terry Walton has established himself as a popular voice on BBC Radio 2, broadcasting from his allotment in the Rhondda Valley on the *Jeremy Vine* show. From the age of four he helped his parents tend their plot, and despite the demands of a career in engineering he's never been without his hillside allotment, which he says has helped him maintain a sense of perspective on the world.

Terry Walton's top 10 tips
Here is some advice about how to get the very best out of your vegetable patch:

1 Size Make it as big as you can, but as much as you can manage. Raised beds look nice, and can be beneficial if you can't bend down or are less able, but they require paths, which means you lose valuable productive space. Aesthetically, raised beds can provide a great design element to a formal garden, and are ideal for containing rampant herbs, such as mint, and cut flowers, but if you're serious about high production, you'll grow more if you plant directly into the ground.

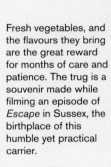

Fresh vegetables, and the flavours they bring are the great reward for months of care and patience. The trug is a souvenir made while filming an episode of *Escape* in Sussex, the birthplace of this humble yet practical carrier.

2 Location Pick the sunniest position you can find; you can always introduce shade if necessary further down the line, and south-facing plots are ideal. You should also aim to have a water source nearby, which will pay dividends during the establishment of young plants. Run-off from a shed or glasshouse is a good way of harvesting water into troughs or butts if you have no mains source available.

3 Prepare the ground well Look after it, and it will look after you. Use plenty of manure, and always rely on organic materials that will build up the fertility using natural organisms. Dig it all in. Find local sources of manure, ideally well-rotted for a minimum of two years. Make sure horse muck is collected from herbicide-free pasture, and avoid stable muck that contains wood chips; stock kept on straw is always a better bet as wood chips reduce nitrogen when it breaks down in the soil.

4 Plan You should plan what to grow based upon varieties you really like. Some crops require rotation, such as potatoes or beans, and will need well-manured soil. In contrast brassicas and cabbages needs lots of lime and a slightly alkaline soil, while root crops such as parsnips and carrots want plain, stone-free soil, not manure based. Succession cropping is also important. For example, with lettuces, only sow six over two weeks, rather than dozens at once, which will only over-supply you and go to waste. The same is true for cabbages, which are also fast growing. Managing your output will mean you only reap what you need, while maintaining a fresh supply.

5 Feeding When crops are growing well, feed at least once a week; seaweed if you can get it, or manure, comfrey and nettles steeped in water is a cheap and effective way of creating your own organic feed. Steeping is easy using a large plastic dustbin with a lid into which you pile the ingredients and fill with water. Once left for around three weeks it will give you a healthy, if slightly pungent, feed, which you can water in through a can with a rose. May or June is a good time for harvesting comfrey or nettles, and if you have a patch of your own you can harvest it again in a further 8–10 weeks, giving you enough to last a year.

6 Be vigilant! When your patch is growing well keep an eye out for pests that'll love your crops as much as you do; aphids will breed fast and decimate any crops as they suck the sap out. Crush them between finger and thumb, or blast them off with clean water from a hand pump sprayer, but avoid pesticides. Carrots can be protected under a fine net to keep carrot root fly at bay, and brassicas will also do well under a net to keep butterflies out.

7 Harvest time Always crop when plants are young and tender, and plan your crops so that you can be supplied all year round. Terry never has to buy veg, so a careful plan to plant salad crops, root vegetables and brassicas should mean you are well stocked through the year.

8 Weeding Always look over your shoulder – keep on top of the weeds, and don't compost perennials such as dandelions and docks, as you'll never get rid of them. Annuals such as bitter cress should be fine to compost. Not only are weeds unsightly, they can also choke young vegetable plants if left to mature, and will take water and nutrients out of your well-prepared soil.

9 Heat and light If possible, have a small glasshouse for bringing on young plants and over-wintering, and a shed for storing summer veg like potatoes, onions and squashes, as well as tools. It will also provide you with a source of water, if you can collect rain from the roof and gutters into a butt.

10 Enjoy! Last but certainly not least, don't lose sight of the fact that it should be a hobby not a job, so enjoy it and have fun! Trying new varieties and methods is the reward that successful vegetable gardeners enjoy, no matter how big or small their plots, and irrespective of experience or expertise.

Terry Walton on his beloved allotment in Wales.

learn to appreciate how hard producing good quality food is, the better. It's great company to be in, which is why it's been in my blood for generations.'

It may be hard work but it'll be hugely rewarding. The benefits for your health will be many-fold too; not least because you should be able to enjoy the advantages of consuming your own produce!

Keeping chickens

Keeping birds for meat or eggs has been a staple of country life for centuries. Geese, turkeys, ducks, guinea fowl and quail are still kept by bird lovers, but the simple business of having a few chickens is a hugely popular aim for those moving to the countryside.

For some it's a chance to rekindle childhood memories of growing up with hens, while for the majority it's an opportunity to dabble in a bit of (very) small-scale farming! We were no different when we moved out to the Welsh Borders. Either way, there is much to recommend eating

truly fresh eggs, laid by birds that you know have been well cared for, and which, importantly, have been fed on food you can trust. Chickens can also make a big contribution to family life; characterful and entertaining, it's easy to while away the time watching them scratch about, while caring for them is good fun and easy to do. They are a great way of introducing children to the responsibilities of looking after animals, and the thrill of opening the egg box to see how many have been laid never leaves you, whatever your age.

If you have never kept chickens before, here are the things you should consider before you start.

Chickens require daily care They need to be let out and fed every day, so you must be prepared for the commitment, and have a friend or neighbour you can rely on should you be away for any period of time.

Space It's important to work out how many hens you need based on the amount of eggs you'd like. We have always found that five is more than enough to supply our family and that of our neighbour who shares in the fun of looking after them. Chickens require roughly a 1ft × 1ft space each within a hen house, and 10 sq. ft outside, but the more you give them the happier they will be. If you are planning on having more than 50 hens though, you'll have to register them as a commercial enterprise.

Far left: My mischievous Labrador Iolo eyes our chickens through the wire of their run. Left: The real prize we all enjoy is the gift of fresh eggs every day.

Security Chickens are extremely vulnerable to predators. Dogs are an obvious problem, but the fox is undoubtedly the master. It is important to create a run for your chickens that is fox-proof, ideally a securely wired enclosure with the fence sunk 1ft below ground to stop the fox tunnelling underneath it, and high enough to stop him jumping over (about 6½ft). Many manage with less fortified areas, but having suffered the sad loss of our small flock to the fox I can only recommend taking as many precautions as you can.

Choosing the hen house Your hens will need a secure house in which to sleep and lay their eggs. They range in size and style from traditional triangular arks, to wheeled houses and modern plastic Eglus that are perfect for smaller gardens and yards. They are fun to design and build either from scratch or by repurposing an existing shelter, but should always be waterproof and windproof, be well ventilated and give you easy access to the nest boxes.

Location You will need to provide your chickens with shelter from the worst of the wind and rain and shade for hot summer days, so deciding where to put your chicken run is important; they can quickly turn into messy muddy areas, but they need not be banished out of sight if done with care and flair. I've seen good examples where the design, materials used and site have combined to make a chicken run that enhances a space, while the more room your chickens have the more content they will be. It's also worth having your run close to a dry store of some sort, where you can keep their feed and the tools needed to muck them out.

Choosing your chickens There are a huge number of breeds to choose from, which will produce different sized and coloured eggs, but you should take advice on which will be the easiest for you to look after, depending on where in the country you are; some will favour warmer and drier climates than others. Increasingly, people are seeking out ex-battery hens, giving them a new free-range life. Roosters (cockerels) are not necessary for hens to lay eggs, but they do add colour and character, while their cry is the unmistakable soundtrack to country life. If you plan to have one, just check your neighbours won't mind beforehand!

Buying your hens You should take great care in choosing your hens – know where they are coming from, and never buy them unseen if you don't know the breeder. It's very easy to buy diseased or sickly birds. Going to see where they are coming from will reassure you they are from a reputable source – one that will also be able to advise you going forward. Hens can live for up to 10 years, but the chances are you'll be replacing them sooner than that.

Routine It's important to establish a simple routine; letting them out in the morning, feeding, mucking out, providing daily fresh water and shutting them safely inside the hen house at night are all essential. Regularly collecting the eggs is one of the rewards of hen-keeping that you can look forward to. Foxes tend to hunt at dusk or at night, but be aware they might start earlier in the winter.

Feed Hens use a huge amount of energy in laying eggs, so proprietary feeds such as layers' pellets or mash are a good way of giving them a balanced diet. They also like green vegetables, nettle tops and grass clippings, while some things like potato skins and broccoli should be boiled beforehand. Most good chicken-keeping handbooks will advise you on a wide range of foods that will both feed and entertain them.

Disease Chickens can suffer with all sorts of unpleasant conditions, but ensuring you keep them as clean and healthy as possible will go a long way to fending off these problems. Red mite is perhaps the most common problem, so regular disinfecting of your hen house while mucking it out will really help, using a product such as Poultry Shield.

GREEN WOODWORKING

One of the great pleasures of making *Escape to the Country* has been the chance to experience a huge range of traditional skills and crafts. Dry-stone walling, thatching, hedge laying or foraging in woodlands and along the shore, are some of the most rewarding ways to spend your free time – or work day if you can make a commercial success out of getting 'hands on'.

Yet of all the traditions I've seen, my affinity for wood struck the strongest chord in the ancient pursuit of green woodworking. Throughout history we have used freshly cut hardwoods to make everything from houses to tables, stools, spoons and a huge array of other everyday household items. Crafting by hand what would otherwise so easily just be firewood into items of great use, value and beauty taps into a primeval instinct to learn and adapt.

The great joy of using green wood is that because it's fresh it's easy to work – so it also lends itself to pieces of art as well as more traditional furniture. This quality is also key to designing and creating bigger items that will be joined together using time-honoured techniques, because the wood will shrink and harden, tightening joints so that they last a lifetime, if done well. These properties were used by 'bodgers' – itinerant chair makers who turned legs on simple pole lathes that go back hundreds if not thousands of years. Today, while there are plenty of mechanical short cuts open to the modern green woodworker, for many there is nothing quite like a piece of furniture or an object created just using traditional tools and methods.

One of the other great joys of working with wood in this way is the people you meet when learning how to do it. I took a course run by an old friend called Sherwood who had his own forest complete with a woodland kitchen! Working in woodland, warmed by your labours, with the sweet smell of a nearby open fire, even in the winter months when green wood is readily harvested, is one of life's great escapes. There is no rush, your time is governed by the season, the weather, who you are with and the object you're making. What's more, you'll also come away with something beautiful and useful.

Making this useful shave horse took me two days and doing so taught me most of the techniques needed by the green wood worker. Basically a large clamp, it's an essential item to have.

A montage of country life. Clockwise from top left: Humour, nurturing a younger generation, the chance to stretch your legs in the great outdoors and enjoying living with animals are just some of the reasons I believe so many of us are drawn to escape the urban sprawl and return to our rural roots.

PART II
EXPLORING THE BRITISH ISLES

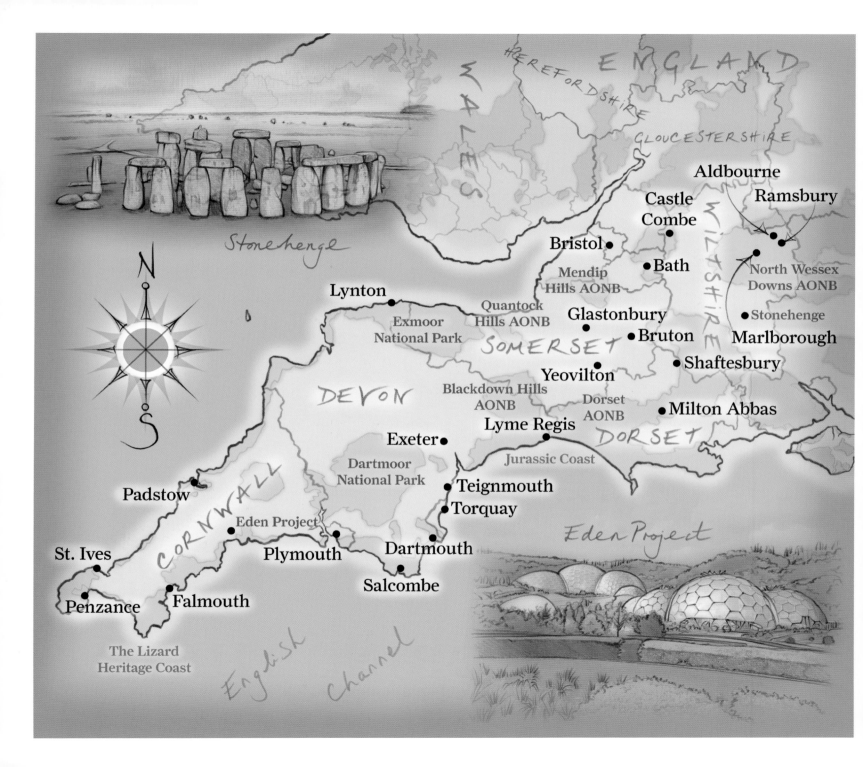

WALES

HEREFORDSHIRE

ENGLAND

GLOUCESTERSHIRE

Aldbourne

Ramsbury

Castle
Combe

Bristol

Bath

North Wessex
Downs AONB

Mendip
Hills AONB

WILTSHIRE

Stonehenge

Quantock
Hills AONB

Glastonbury

Bruton

Marlborough

Lynton

Exmoor
National Park

SOMERSET

Yeovilton

Shaftesbury

DEVON

Blackdown Hills
AONB

Dorset
AONB

Milton Abbas

Lyme Regis

DORSET

Exeter

Jurassic Coast

Dartmoor
National Park

Teignmouth

Torquay

Eden Project

Padstow

Eden Project

Dartmouth

St. Ives

Plymouth

Salcombe

Penzance

Falmouth

CORNWALL

The Lizard
Heritage Coast

English

Channel

Stonehenge

The West Country

The South West of England is probably the most popular region in the UK for those wishing to Escape to the Country, combining the gems of Wiltshire, Somerset, Dorset, Devon and of course Cornwall.

From Somerset's mysterious Levels, to Devon's Dartmoor and Cornwall's rugged and enchanting coastlines, the South West really does have something for everyone, with a wide range of landscapes and property to furnish you with the lifestyle of your choice. Whether you fancy upland, inland or coastal, or something within the great National Parks of either Dartmoor or Exmoor, you'll be spoilt for choice. There are a host of Areas of Outstanding Natural Beauty (AONBs) that you can also pick from, such as the Blackdown Hills of Somerset.

Somerset

I've always seen Somerset as a county of quarters; in the north it's serviced by the great maritime city of Bristol, south of which the uplands of the Mendip Hills provide the bedrock to prehistoric Cheddar Gorge, and overlook the sprawling, peat-filled Levels, which surround the world-famous Tor at Glastonbury.

Perched upon its glacial hill, Glastonbury Tor is one of the most famous landmarks in the British landscape. It has, over many years, become an old friend that I still love to see, either up close after a climb to its summit, or via a distant glimpse through the mist that often swirls above these ancient wetlands and which only adds to the abundance of Arthurian legends that continue to cast their spell today.

Left: In Somerset the astonishing landscape of Cheddar Gorge is on your doorstep and the caves that lie within are equally as breathtaking.

Right: Bruton in Somerset attracts a sophisticated crowd with its world-renowned art gallery, Hauser & Wirth, independent shops and restaurants. There is also a direct train service to and from London.

To the west of Somerset's county town of Taunton, the Quantocks border the coast of the Bristol Channel to the north and the vast expanse of Exmoor to the west notable, among other things, for the ponies that have roamed the moorland for thousands of years. These rambling hills are one of my favourite parts of the county, yet are often overlooked by house hunters. Seemingly remote, it's easy to get lost in their sunken lanes and forgotten villages, yet this area still enjoys quick access to the M5 and the railway stations along the South West mainline, which connects Bristol to Penzance via Exeter.

To the south and east, Somerset takes in the gentle landscapes that surround Yeovilton and gems like Bruton, a timeless village with some breathtaking architecture, and goes on to border the splendour of Dorset's rolling hills. Boasting over 10,000 listed buildings and 500 ancient monuments, Somerset is recognised by those seeking a rural life as a beautiful county with a deep sense of enchantment and mystical history.

Dorset

Dorset has few rivals when it comes to our picture of the quintessential English landscape that its geology, soils and climate have combined over millennia to create. Great bulbous downs sweep around its fertile lowlands and the ancient town of Shaftesbury, while its famous Jurassic coastline has inspired generations of fossil hunters. Lyme Regis is one of my favourite coastal haunts, inspiring too the pen of author John Fowles who famously used it as the setting for the *French Lieutenant's Woman*. When it comes to pretty villages Dorset will not let you down; Milton Abbas, for example, lined with thatch and limestone cottages, has made Dorset a favourite among our buyers and film crews. The county's rich history is dominated by the remains of Britain's largest Iron Age hillfort at Maiden Castle, famously besieged by the Romans around AD 43. This stunning location was made much of in the 1967 film adaptation of Dorset's own Thomas Hardy's *Far from the Madding Crowd*. If, like many, you want access to the coast, beautiful landscapes, classic country property, and a feeling that you really have left the hustle and bustle behind you (Dorset is the only county in England that doesn't have a motorway running through it) then Dorset should definitely be on the list of places in which to find your new rural retreat.

Right above: The natural limestone arch on the Jurassic coast at Durdle Door, near Lulworth, in Dorset is one of the region's most famous landmarks.

Right below: Milton Abbas in Dorset consists of 36 thatched cottages made from cob; they were originally built to house two families each.

Hambledon Hill in Dorset is an Iron Age hillfort in the Blackmore Vale. From the summit of this chalk outcrop that stands at 630ft, on a clear day you can see three counties: Dorset, Somerset and Wiltshire.

Just a mile to the west of the pretty and popular coastal town of Lynton in Devon is the surreal and uncompromising Valley of the Rocks. I first came here a decade ago in a howling gale that only compounded the mystery and majesty of the place. Formed from Devonian rock some 400 million years old, the valley formations set against the backdrop of the Bristol Channel appear to have been strewn about the place by quarrelling giants. Today the giants are long gone, leaving only a herd of feral goats to graze its enchanting slopes.

Alternative locations to Dorset

North Devon Dorset has long been one of my favourite counties, but its popularity comes at a price. Consider instead North Devon, which will allow you to stay in the South West, and offer plenty of dramatic coastline, with the added bonus of the Exmoor National Park on your doorstep.

Wiltshire Wiltshire has the advantage of being within easy reach of London, Bristol and Oxford, in particular the swathe around Marlborough known as the North Wessex Downs. While it is hard to choose between the riches of this ancient and beautiful county, this area that takes in the thatched gems of Ramsbury and Aldbourne is one of my favourite haunts. Prices here are still high, but certainly better value for money than the Cotswolds just to the north.

Long hailed as the prettiest village in England, Castle Combe is packed with some of the best examples of distinctive Cotswold architecture. The honey-coloured stone cottages and town houses, along with its fifteenth-century church, are a testament to its success as a cloth weaving centre that thrived during Henry V's wars with France.

The village of Avebury in Wiltshire lies within the Stonehenge and Avebury World Heritage Site which is recognised for its Neolithic and Bronze Age monuments. The stone circle – the largest in the world with a diameter of 460ft– and huge banks and ditches of the man-made henge that surrounds it were constructed around 4,300 years ago. It has long been a favourite of mine, not least because you can still wander freely among the stones of this captivating wonder of the ancient world.

Devon

Devon holds court as the most popular of the *Escape to the Country* destinations. Broadly divided into south and north it's the only county in England that enjoys two coastlines. To the north, rugged stretches around Hartland Point face the Atlantic approaches and have been battered into some of the most dramatic coastal views in the country.

By contrast the southern, more sheltered, areas around Teignmouth, Salcombe and Dartmouth are a calmer offering, looking out across the English Channel, and very popular with holidaymakers keen to make the best of some fabulous weather and sparkling waters. Inland, Dartmoor's brooding and prehistoric landscape makes it one of Britain's most popular National Parks, complete with hordes of wild ponies grazing among the rocky outcrops, and tors that have inspired poets, artists and writers for years. Sir Arthur Conan Doyle's infamous hound of the Baskervilles can almost be heard howling across the moors on foggy winter nights. Villages such as Lustleigh and Moretonhampstead feel lost in time among the sweeping moors and sunken lanes, which give the region a truly unique feel.

Aside from the beautiful landscapes, Devon also boasts Europe's oldest cinema; the Torbay Picture House, which is over 100 years old!

Opposite: Dartmoor ponies grazing on Sheep's Tor in the Dartmoor National Park, Devon.

Left above: Salcombe is one of the prettiest towns in South Devon. The streets are lined with art galleries, shops and restaurants, while the sheltered waters make it a perfect place for watersports.

Left below: Woolacombe in North Devon, seen here from Morte Point, is a large, lively village that is popular with homeowners and holidaymakers alike.

Cornwall

It is estimated that five million tourists flock to Cornwall each year, inspired by its coastline, tiny, timeless fishing villages such as Port Isaac, and international attractions like the Eden Project. Its rich industrial history from tin mining, seen in the countless chimneys that dot the landscape, to the vast china clay quarries that furnished the tables of the nation with crockery, Cornwall's story occupies an important slice of the nation's history.

Cornwall's unique climate, with air warmed by the Gulf Stream, has also furnished it with a mouth-watering selection of gardens; the once lost gardens at Heligan and the tropical haven of Trebah being among my favourites. Coastal hotspots such as Falmouth, Padstow and the artistic mecca of St Ives, which hosts a Tate Gallery, represent for many visitors the value of the county not just as a place in which to holiday, but increasingly also a place in which to live.

Yet in many ways Cornwall is something of a contradiction. People are drawn to the surfing beaches and 433 miles of coastline (the longest of any county in England), meaning that tourism now accounts for around a third of its income, but it has long been an area that has struggled economically. The result is that while property premiums can be astronomical around the main centres, not least those on the coast, inland prices can fall away sharply.

Left: Levant Mine and Beam Engine, Cornwall. High on the cliffs overlooking the Atlantic, Levant was one of Cornwall's champion mines for over 100 years.

Right: The twisting lanes and beautiful sheltered harbour of Port Isaac have also been the backdrop to ITV's *Doc Martin*, and most recently the hit film *Fisherman's Friends*, based upon the true story of Port Isaac's shanty men whose distinctive sound propelled them into the UK music charts a decade ago.

Sadly, many communities that thrive in the summer months now suffer off-season because of the surge in second homes that, while satisfying the holiday market, have also put many properties out of reach for locals and incomers who want a place in which to live all year round and who are perhaps trying to get on the property ladder for the first time with limited budgets. Seasonal extremes in the economy are well worth considering if you've fallen in love with a county you've only seen while on holiday. You may find that come the long months of winter, what you thought was a vibrant and exciting place to live may become anything but as it hibernates off-season with a corresponding lack of local services and community.

Right: Padstow is a working fishing port at the head of the Camel River. Famously put on the map by chef Rick Stein, it has long been popular with tourists and locals alike, drawn to the bright sand and turquoise waters that grace it during the summer months.

Below right: Pentire Farm on the Pentire Headland in Cornwall. The headland overlooks Polzeath, a small village on the opposite side of the Camel estuary to Padstow with a rich history and literary connections.

Left: St Michael's Mount was originally the site of a Benedictine Priory, and is accessed by a causeway at low tide and by ferry at high tide. Topped by a medieval church and castle dating from the twelfth century, the island is home to a community of about 30 and the St Aubyn family, who have owned it since the seventeenth century.

Alternative locations to Cornwall

Cornwall may be one of the most aspirational places to escape to but prices on the coast are always going to include a premium that can be at odds with the realities of life in a place that is often seasonal. So, if coast and raw countryside are for you, but you need to be within four hours of London, or indeed the rest of the country, think about Pembrokeshire and neighbouring Ceredigion in West Wales. You'll get affordability with a choice, it's alive all year round and some of Britain's best beaches and attractions are on hand too.

Above: Treleddyd Fawr Cottage has undergone painstaking and sympathetic restoration by the National Trust for Wales. It is now a holiday let, so you too can experience what life was like in one of the last surviving traditional cottages in Pembrokeshire.

Left: Haven Point, Pembrokeshire. The Pembrokeshire coast offers unspoiled beaches and stunning scenery, plus a great range of architectural treats, from farm and manor houses to cosy cottages. What's more, the seasonal extremes felt in other high tourist areas are less of an issue.

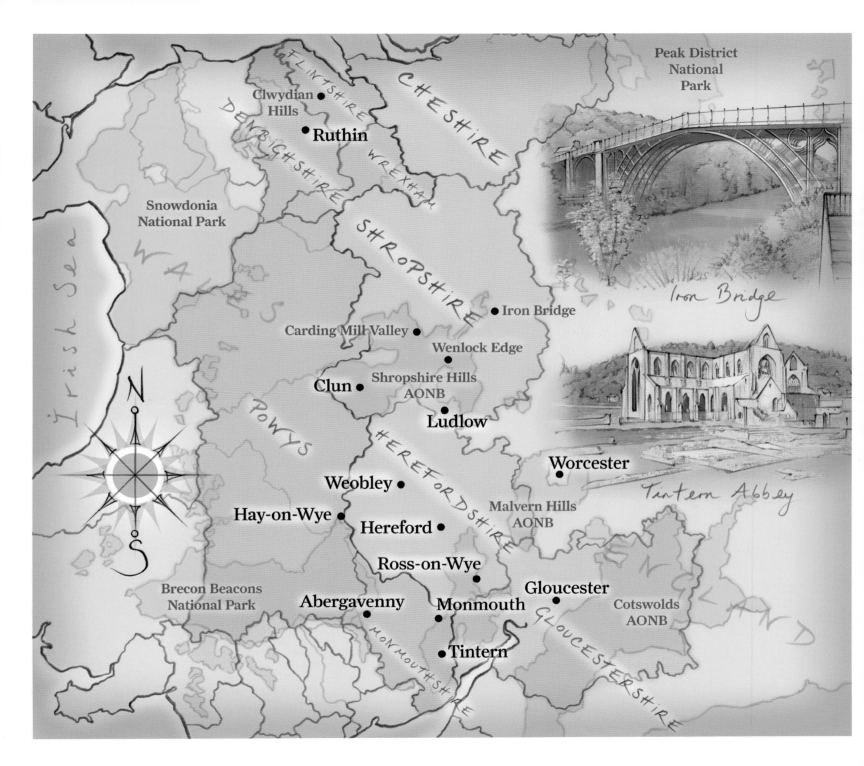

Peak District National Park

CHESHIRE

Clwydian Hills

● **Ruthin**

FLINTSHIRE

DENBIGHSHIRE

WREXHAM

Snowdonia National Park

STROPSHIRE

WALES

Irish Sea

● Iron Bridge

Carding Mill Valley ●

Wenlock Edge

Clun ●

Shropshire Hills AONB

POWYS

● **Ludlow**

HEREFORDSHIRE

N

S

Weobley ●

Malvern Hills AONB

● **Worcester**

Hay-on-Wye ●

Hereford ●

Ross-on-Wye
●

Brecon Beacons National Park

● **Gloucester**

Cotswolds AONB

Abergavenny

Monmouth

MONMOUTHSHIRE

ENGLAND

GLOUCESTERSHIRE

● **Tintern**

Iron Bridge

Tintern Abbey

The Welsh Borders

For me, there are few more diverse or inspiring parts of the country than the Welsh Borders that stretch from the Severn Estuary in the south, to the River Dee in the north. Today, these once hotly contested borderlands are made up of Monmouthshire, Herefordshire, Shropshire and in part Wrexham, Cheshire, Denbighshire and Flintshire. They offer a great stepping-off point for any Welsh adventure, and as a region it benefits from being relatively underpopulated. Living here also means you're well connected to the rest of the country too. From top to bottom, airports in Manchester, Birmingham, Bristol and Cardiff are comfortably within a couple of hours and, if you need it, London is possible in around three hours by either car or train.

For many who have not been as lucky as I have to travel extensively around the UK, the Welsh Borders are often not even known let alone considered. For decades now the South West of England has become entrenched as the urban escapees' default, but take it from someone who has travelled widely throughout the area and now lives here, you're missing out on a well-connected yet wonderfully rural gem of a region that's steeped in history and swathed in glorious countryside, and one that really does offer something for everyone.

A bloody history

Like most borders throughout history, these have seen their fair share of political, economic and military upheaval. Since prehistoric times this natural fault line between what we now know as England and Wales has in part been defined by the regional geography that has helped establish the cultural distinctions found on both sides. The natural boundaries of the rivers Dee and Severn, along with the creation of the astonishing earthwork of Offa's Dyke during the latter half of the eighth century have all determined that what are now some of the country's most beautiful counties were once some of the bloodiest. Often referred to as the Welsh Marches, following the Norman conquest of 1066 successive kings from William the Conqueror onwards conferred great power on their 'Marcher' Lords. Armed with Royal assent it was they who reigned with virtual autonomy over this restless region with steely purpose and a casual brutality, both fortifying the line and from here launching military forays into Wales itself. It is perhaps no surprise that the region boasts a huge number of castles and earlier hillforts that remain to remind us of this turbulent past.

The Georgian splendour of Dunham Massey
in Cheshire; red brick architecture is a feature of
the northern borders, from stately homes to
farmhouses and cottages.

Architectural gems

Architecturally the region boasts some of the finest country property in the UK, from the stone-built cottages of the lower Wye Valley in and around Tintern and Monmouth through to the famous 'Black and White' timber-framed beauties that can be found throughout Herefordshire, Shropshire and Cheshire, itself also notable for a huge number of beautiful red-brick farmhouses and halls such as Dunham Massey. More urban hotspots include Monmouth, the book town of Hay and riverside Ross-on-Wye, Ledbury and more centrally Ludlow, often championed as the food capital of England and a place rich in architecture and history, its medieval and Georgian streets overlooked by the striking castle. County towns such as Shrewsbury and Chester complete the picture but there are numerous villages and smaller towns tucked away such as Clun, vibrant Church Stretton and the picturesque Ruthin in Denbighshire, all of which would invite a stop and add much colour and texture to any adventure as you border-hop either side from south to north.

Right above: The old packhorse bridge at Clun in Shropshire dates from 1450. The town grew up around its Saxon church built in the seventh century, but there has been a settlement in this area since the Neolithic period.

Right below: The county town of Shrewsbury lies on the banks of the River Severn. With over 600 listed buildings its architecture includes a Norman castle, a Benedictine monastery, Tudor and Georgian townhouses and the Ditherington Flax Mill built in the late eighteenth century, which is regarded as a precursor to the skyscraper.

Inspiring landscape

The landscapes along this fascinating ribbon have for years inspired artists and poets, not least the Wye Valley and its links to both J. M. W. Turner and Wordsworth. The poet A. E. Housman described Shropshire as a 'county for easy livers, the quietist under the sun'. Since 1958 the stunning Shropshire Hills have been designated an Area of Outstanding Natural Beauty (AONB) as anyone who's taken the time to explore the dramatic Carding Mill Valley and summit the Long Mynd will tell you. These uplands also boast the Stiper Stones: one of the most emotive points in the Shropshire Hills they include 'The Devil's Chair'. When covered in low cloud and mist, it is said the Devil himself is in residence, while further north the prehistoric hillforts of the Clwydian Hills offer fantastic views towards Snowdonia in the west and Cheshire to the east.

It is without doubt the huge range of architecture, history, landscapes and space that has long singled out the Welsh Borders as one of my favourite parts of the British Isles, so much so that since 2012 they've been my home too. So, if you are thinking of making the move here, I can heartily recommend it.

Herefordshire

Weobley

Few villages in England have claimed so many prizes over the years as Weobley. Be it 'Best-kept Village', one of the finest in which to live or indeed to visit before you die, Weobley continues to revel in them all. At every turn you'll be met with yet another stunning example of historic timber-framed architecture, which makes this tiny village and the county of Herefordshire as a whole so distinctive. To walk its streets is to wander through a catalogue of medieval timber-framed design, where crucks, jetties, pargetting and fine carving will immerse the architectural historian in the sense that this tiny settlement with its towering church and ruined castle really has been left behind by the modern world.

Below: There is an unmistakable outline to the Shropshire Hills that cluster around the popular border town of Church Stretton.

Right: Weobley in Herefordshire, with its array of half-timbered buildings, is regarded by many as one of the most attractive villages in the UK.

Shropshire

Ludlow

I first stumbled across Ludlow in Shropshire in the early days of *Escape to the Country* over a decade ago. As the series developed and we championed yet more locations in the Welsh Borders the region became something of a second home for me until we moved here ourselves. Ludlow itself is one of the prettiest and most popular market towns in the country and with good reason. Founded by the Norman De Lacy family in 1086 when they set about building not just the castle but a planned town to go with it, over the centuries its position has ensured steady economic development within an original grid system, which is easily recognised. Today the town's streets are lined with some 500 listed buildings, from stunning timber-framed houses to elegant Georgian and Victorian gems. In its heyday during the early nineteenth century Ludlow was known for its glove-making industry but a slump in its economic fortunes in the first half of the twentieth century ensured that it did not suffer great redevelopment, with the result that it now remains one of the best-preserved towns in the country. Long famous as a tourist destination and foodie hotspot it has become a popular stepping-off point for many exploring the region for the first time, and it remains a huge draw for those looking to buy within its magical orbit.

Opposite and above: The Abergavenny Food Festival. If Ludlow has been known as the food capital of England thanks to the once high number of Michelin-starred restaurants it boasted, the reinvention of the Welsh market town of Abergavenny as a foodie destination has only confirmed what many who live here have long known. High-quality artisan producers of beef, lamb, cheese, cider and now wine have established the region as a real gastronomic hotspot for visitors and locals alike.

Right above: Looking south from the Malvern Hills in Worcestershire. The hills also lie within the counties of Herefordshire and a small part of Gloucestershire. As well as offering stunning views the area is of great geological and ecological importance.

Right below: At the end of the eighteenth century the great iron master Abraham Darby III was commissioned to build a bridge of iron, the first of its kind in the world. The Iron Bridge built in 1779 is today rightly recognised as one of the wonders of the Industrial Revolution.

TIMBER FRAMING

The techniques and materials used in the construction of timber-framed buildings are as old as most of the timbers themselves, stretching back well over 1,000 years. The vast majority you'll see, be they in the Welsh Borders, East Anglia, Dorset, Kent or Sussex to highlight just some of the main hotspots, will have been built from oak. When felled and still relatively moist, it's known as 'green oak', and is easy to cut and work. However, once it dries it becomes incredibly strong and virtually impervious to anything except a modern drill bit. The curing of such an organic material will often cause it to shrink, twist and crack or shear, lending an idiosyncratic shape and form to many timber-framed buildings with their wonky walls and floors.

Over the last 40 years there has been a steady resurgence of building in green oak, and a welcome revival of many of the old skills and tools required. It should come as no surprise that this should have begun in the oak-framed heartland of the Welsh Borders. Now based in the Herefordshire village of Kingsland, Border Oak was originally set up by passionate oak-wright and builder John Green, and has since established itself as the market leader, once again building from scratch manor houses, cottages, barns, stables and outbuildings just as our medieval predecessors did. Many others have now followed suit, such as Welsh Oak, Oakwrights and Wye Oak to mention just a few, but the results are stunning. Not only do you get a new-build, which by default is oozing with character, you are getting one which can celebrate the past while embracing the future in a suite of designs that combine the best of tradition with the very latest mod-cons. What's more they are extremely well insulated using a range of modern materials to replicate traditional wattle and daub, and they are all designed to breathe, creating homes that will last and belong in a landscape, which has both created and shaped them. My own house was built in 1580, but if I were starting from scratch I'd go for green oak in a heartbeat, happy in the knowledge that the home I was creating would doubtless be around in another 500 years.

Right: Ludlow's wealth of Tudor and timber façades has long established it as one of the principal architectural gems of the Welsh Borders, and a great market town in which to live.

Left: Medieval timber-framed buildings along Grope Lane in Shrewsbury.

Right: Herefordshire boasts a 'black and white trail' for those with a keen eye to soak up the timber framed splendour of hotspots, such as Pembridge, Leominster and here in ever-popular Weobley.

The wonderful Wye Valley

The Wye Valley has long been celebrated as one of the most picturesque pockets in the UK, and with good reason. In 1782 the Reverend William Gilpin, doubtless inspired by the local popularity of the Wye Valley coined the word 'picturesque' in what is now recognised as the first tour guide published in Britain. *Observations on the River Wye and Several Parts of South Wales* became a bestseller and established the term 'picturesque' in describing a version of the perfect landscape inspired by the artists of the day. His work accelerated the development of the Wye Valley from Ross to Chepstow as a popular tourist destination by the early 1800s.

The drama of the Wye Gorge at Symonds Yat, and the rolling lowlands through which the river meanders, taking in numerous ruins such as Goodrich Castle and Tintern Abbey drew in artists, poets and romantics from around the world. Today the Wye Valley remains one of the nation's most treasured landscapes, and has for many come to define what the southern reaches of the Welsh Borders have to offer, from stunning and varied scenery scattered with pretty market towns, to villages and a rich array of historic architecture. For over 200 years the valley has cast a spell upon all those who have pottered along the winding river, exuding a magic that time has not diminished.

The dramatic heights of the Wye Gorge contrast with the rolling hills and rich pasture of the lowlands that in turn escort the River Wye on its passage through southern Herefordshire, Monmouthshire and Gloucestershire.

Above: The view from Symonds Yat Rock. This renowned viewpoint in the Wye Valley overlooks a spectacular gorge famous for its nesting peregrine falcons and other raptors, while this stretch of the wye itself is hugely popular with canoeists.

Opposite: Tintern Abbey. 'A more pleasing retreat could not easily be found': 200 years later, it's hard not to agree with the words of eighteenth-century artist William Gilpin.

Surrey to Shropshire

For some buyers, retiring is an opportunity to upsize as we found during a memorable house hunt in Shropshire.

Allan and Lorraine took the unusual decision to upsize when they moved to retire, so that the whole extended family could come and stay for longer.

In the summer of 2018, Allan and Lorraine from Haslemere in Surrey joined Margherita Taylor to find their ideal Escape to the Country in Shropshire. With a budget of £425,000 they were looking for a rural retreat that would notably see them bucking the trend of many retirees to downsize, preferring instead to buy a slightly bigger home so that their grown-up children with growing families would have plenty of space when they came to visit. With a passion for gardening and dogs, they also wanted a property that would match their outdoor ambitions, which included vegetable gardening and having chickens, and while they were keen to find something they could

famously 'put their stamp on', they did not want to take on a major project. Yet after some 37 years in the same house, this was a move that represented a huge emotional transition, one which would require them to fall head over heels in love with a new home that would replace their existing one.

In many respects, they were representative of many buyers we meet; their budget was in line with the series average for many at retirement age, and they were not trying to fulfil an overly ambitious wish-list. In short, a pretty, characterful property set within glorious countryside that would give them three or four bedrooms and spacious living areas was all that was

required, with a manageable garden and if possible existing workshop space or room in which they could build one.

Having viewed three viable options, they eventually picked the first property Margherita showed them, and they moved in just three months after seeing it. Priced at £415,000 it was comfortably under budget and was eventually secured for £405,000.

In the early summer of 2019 I caught up with them to see how they were getting along. Their old life in Haslemere is fast becoming a distant memory and they have rapidly created a rural lifestyle that has become all-embracing. With a few minor changes the house itself has provided a perfect fit for them and their growing extended family, and which has allowed them to pour heart and soul into making the garden and outdoor space very much their own. Blessed with glorious views over Shropshire, they have wasted no time in becoming a welcome addition to the neighbourhood, and have learned much from their new community that has boosted their existing enthusiasm and flair for gardening.

The results are clear to see, as is the sense that they have embraced a lifestyle entirely of their own making. Not only have they succeeded in creating a bigger home in which the whole family can gather throughout the year, they also now enjoy far more quality time with each other because the family can now stay for longer. The emotional hurdle of moving from the home they had known for so long was eased by furnishing their new one with many favoured items from their last: 'We were worried about how we would feel in a different property, but in truth placing our treasured pieces of furniture and other items within a new setting has not only given them a new lease of life, it has also meant we have filled a bigger property with those things that have always made our house a home. We've brought memories with us, but we are now also making many more in a place that already feels like we have been here forever.'

The plunging contours of the Shropshire Hills above the Carding Mill Valley frame the market town of Church Stretton, a popular base for many *Escape to the Country* house hunts over the years.

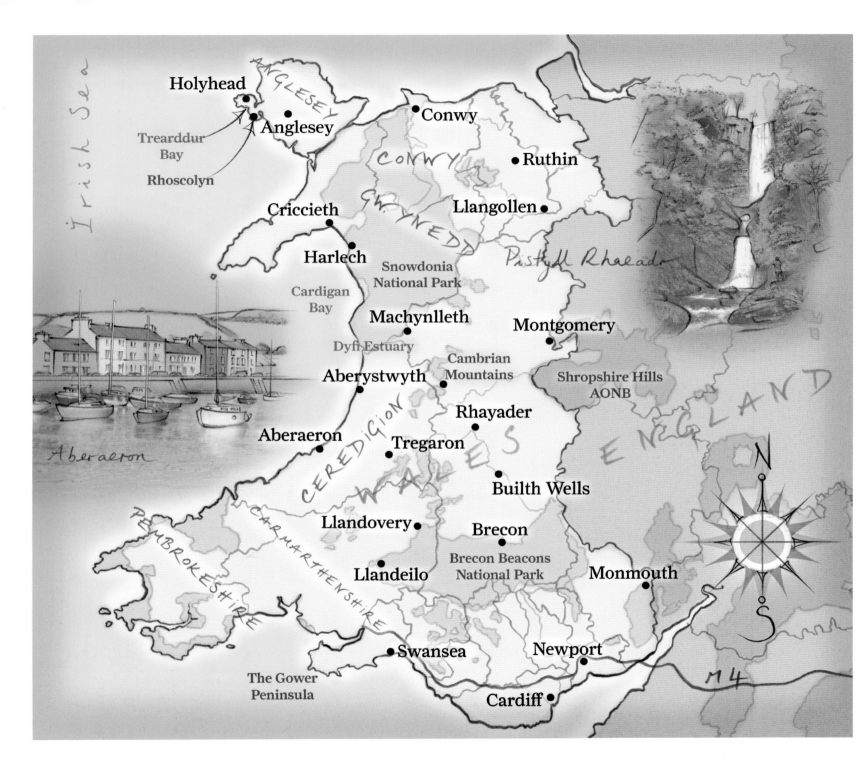

Holyhead

ANGLESEY

Trearddur
Bay

Rhoscolyn

Anglesey

Irish Sea

Conwy

CONWY

Ruthin

GWYNEDD

Llangollen

Criccieth

Pistyll Rhaeadr

Harlech

Snowdonia
National Park

Cardigan
Bay

Machynlleth

Montgomery

Dyfi Estuary

Cambrian
Mountains

Shropshire Hills
AONB

Aberystwyth

CEREDIGION

Rhayader

ENGLAND

Aberaeron

Aberaeron

Tregaron

WALES

Builth Wells

PEMBROKESHIRE

CARMARTHENSHIRE

Llandovery

Brecon

Monmouth

Llandeilo

Brecon Beacons
National Park

N

The Gower
Peninsula

Swansea

Newport

S

Cardiff

M4

Wales

For over half my life, I was proud to call West Wales my home. I first experienced life in the Cambrian Mountains as a 19 year old, and for the following 23 years I came to know it extremely well. From the wilds of upland Ceredigion to the coastline of Cardigan Bay, the heights of Snowdonia, the industrialised valleys of the south and the beauty of the Gower or the unique island pocket of Anglesey, it is a country rich in history, humour, landscapes, culture and property and that I often refer to as my spiritual home.

Wales is often thought of as a nation of farmers, where the population of sheep outnumbers the three million people by three to one. To the north of the once thriving industrial coal-mining corridor that flanks the modern M4 motorway and the capital Cardiff, are three of the most popular National Parks in the UK; Pembrokeshire, the Brecon Beacons and the unmistakable mountains of Snowdonia. In between these diverse landscapes lowlands and uplands interconnect across a country that boasts a broad range of architectural styles drawn from the abundant sources of stone, slate and other raw materials that later industrialisation exploited throughout its history. Moving inland, Ruthin, Llangollen, Montgomery, Brecon, Monmouth and Carmarthen are all market towns that provide good hubs from which to house hunt and eventually live, while coastal favourites such as Pembroke, Aberaeron, Aberystwyth, Conwy, Criccieth and Caernarfon also make great places to begin your journey into home owning in this unique principality.

Value and variety

From classic stone-built cottages up in the mountains, to coastal farmsteads that might make an income through holiday lets or glamping, to many the picture of a rural hideaway built from materials hewn from the landscape is one of the great draws. Whatever your budget, the Welsh rural property market is one in which you shouldn't have to break the bank to find an option that will work. What's more, you will find a sincere welcome within communities that have long been a mix of locals and incomers, and who share in a sense of belonging that draws upon centuries of proud cultural identity. House prices across Wales compare favourably with other parts of the UK; properties with land, views and often great character are within reach of most budgets. When it comes to value for money, it's a country not to be overlooked, and for those keen on smallholdings, it's an excellent place to start your search.

A fortified nation

Wales's chequered political history has left its mark upon the landscape in the many castles that survive as a lasting testament to centuries of conflict. The country now boasts more castles per head of population than anywhere else in the world. Welsh lords were fortifying their bases of power long before the Norman Conquest sought to dilute their authority, while later Norman nobles sought to do the same, but it was the thirteenth-century conquest of Wales by Edward I that brought about one of the greatest fortification programmes in history, that lasted decades and all but bankrupted the Crown. Determined to finally quell Wales after successive rebellions, Edward set about creating a ring of castles that would effectively contain his rebellious subjects. Most were sited on the coasts so that they could be supplied by sea if besieged while others, sited inland, employed the latest architectural devices to ensure they could be defended with a minimum of troops. Of these, the great edifice of Carreg Cennen outside Llandeilo is one of the finest, while the coastal towns of Pembroke, Cardigan, Harlech, Caernarfon and Conwy, to name but a few, still retain the great fortresses that helped establish them as thriving settlements and market towns of today, their modern street plans often reflecting their medieval origins.

A nation of parks

Soon after the tumultuous events of the Second World War, Britain embarked upon a programme that would eventually lead to the creation of 15 National Parks, three of which cover some of the most beautiful landscapes in Wales, if not the UK. Among the first was that in Snowdonia, established in the first wave back in 1951, along with Dartmoor and the Lake District. However, by 1957, Pembrokeshire and the unmistakable heights of the Brecon Beacons had been added to the list. Alongside the Beacons, the 31,000 acres of the Sennybridge Training Area (requisitioned at the start of the war in 1939) provide some of the most important habitats in the UK for a huge range of species of animals and plants. Combined with its stunning coastline, now enshrined in the 870-mile (1,400-km) Welsh Coastal Path, which runs from Chepstow in the south to Queensferry in the north, the opportunities Wales offers to get out and enjoy the great outdoors remain a huge draw for tourists and locals alike. Property prices within its National Parks don't necessarily attract the premiums you might find in areas such as Exmoor or the Lake District, but planning conditions within the boundaries of the parks can, understandably, be quite rigorous.

The view looking east from summit of Corn Du towards Pen y Fan in the Brecon Beacons, Wales.

Anglesey

I've always had a soft spot for this characterful island just off the north coast of Wales. Head into its heart via one of two marvels of the industrial age; either Thomas Telford's early nineteenth-century suspension bridge or Robert Stephenson's later rail and now road bridge, and you'll soon find yourself in a place imbued with a sense of identity that only island life can conjure. From almost everywhere on the island you get a view – looking south of the entire Snowdonian range that sweeps across the horizon from the Carneddau Mountains above Conwy in the east to the sprawling reach of the Llyn Peninsula to the west. Surrounded by a real mix of dramatic rocky coastline and wide beaches, what the island lacks in characterful architecture it more than makes up for in the mix of coast and country that it offers, while giving you ready access to Snowdonia. What's more, while prices are higher in popular holiday hotspots such as Trearddur Bay or Rhoscolyn, across the island property in general can be very affordable.

Llangollen

This tiny town that straddles the River Dee has been a popular haunt of travellers for centuries. The bridge at its heart established its strategic importance, evidenced by the towering ruins of Castell Dinas Brân that are perched on the heights of the surrounding hills. Historically its position on the arterial A5 that connected London to Holyhead and the shipping routes to Ireland also helped it develop into what is now a delightful picture of Victorian and late Georgian architecture grafted onto this ancient North Welsh valley. Today it is also home not only to a particularly fine steam railway, but also to the Welsh National Eisteddfod, the annual music, dance and literary festival that is one of Wales's principal cultural events.

Below: The River Dee that cuts through the centre of Llangollen has long defined it as one of my favourite Welsh market towns, with easy access to Snowdonia, Cheshire and Shropshire.

Above: The Neolithic chambered tomb of Bryn Celli Ddu first took me to Anglesey when I was a student. It's been an old friend ever since.

The Dyfi Estuary is a magical boundary that separates North and Mid Wales through its natural fault line. At its mouth the colourful terraces of Aberdyfi, seen here, overlook the ancient dunes at Ynyslas. At its eastern end the medieval political centre of Machynlleth is typical of many towns in the region, with its mixture of stone and later Victorian architecture. The Dyfi Estuary is recognised as a unique habitat for huge numbers of wading birds and other wildfowl that thrive on the mud flats and salt marshes.

Aberaeron

Aberaeron on the west coast is another of my favourite haunts. Its layout and architecture is unlike many other coastal towns in Wales; the town and port was only begun in 1805. As a relative historic newcomer, Aberaeron's distinctive multi-coloured houses arranged around the harbour and a charming Regency Square set it apart both in style and flavour. Today it's hugely popular among both locals and tourists who swell the population at festivals and events throughout the year. It's a fantastic base from which to house hunt too, with a good range of options for eating and sleeping, not least the Harbour Master Hotel, one of the best in Wales.

A relatively new town, Aberaeron's distinctive, multicoloured terraces give its harbourside a unique backdrop, which has helped ensure its continuing popularity.

The road to Abergwesyn

The upland road that connects the small market town of Tregaron to Beulah outside Builth Wells is one of the most beautiful in the UK, with breathtaking views at every turn. For 27 miles it twists and bucks its way across some of the most dramatic country you'll find. This was one of the main routes that the old drovers used to move their stock to the markets of London, a journey that would have taken weeks but which helped establish tiny settlements like Abergwesyn itself along the way. Properties along this road still occasionally come up for sale. When I meet couples house hunting who complain that having a shop a mile away in Sussex makes them feel too remote, I often picture those living along this ancient trackway, and smile.

Over many years, we have helped numerous buyers realise their hopes of finding a home here, many of whom have been drawn to its scope for smallholders keen to lead a greener life. Some have come with ambitions to be farmers, while others have sought nothing more than a pretty home and to be immersed in its captivating landscapes. Yet common to them all has been the realisation that rural living here can provide a markedly different pace of life to other, more easterly counties, one that really can ring the changes from one lifestyle to another without costing a fortune.

The road to Abergwesyn – an ancient drovers' track and one of the most beautiful roads in Wales.

The unmistakable outline of Craig Goch, one of six dams in the Elan Valley near Rhayader, overflowing after winter rains. These dams still supply the city of Birmingham 73 miles away, through a series of gravity-fed pipes.

The Elenydd, Wales's 'Green Desert'

It is remarkable to anyone who has spent time in the Cambrian Mountains that they have not become a National Park, despite attempts in the early 1970s to have them recognised as such. Today this huge upland swathe of Mid Wales is largely untroubled by tourists; it is quite possible to walk its ridges and steep valleys for days and not see a soul. For 20 years they were my home and I loved them precisely because they were off the beaten track. The few farmsteads that are dotted around them are home to a unique and hardy folk, who, while happy to revel in their splendid isolation, also share a real sense of identity and fellowship with their neighbours, and I always found a warm welcome. The high rainfall here made the Cambrians the ideal host for the capacious Elan Valley Dams, built in the 1890s to provide water for Birmingham, which they still do through a 73-mile, gravity-fed pipe that connects them to the city. The high rainfall also resulted in the source of two of the region's greatest rivers, the Wye and the Severn, which spring from the slopes of the Cambrians' highest peak, Pumlumon.

Yet despite the wind and the rain that is such a feature of this incomparably beautiful landscape, it has long been known as Wales's Green Desert. However, it is not entirely barren; the small market towns that surround it such as Rhayader, Llandovery and Tregaron support many, even smaller, former drovers' villages like Cwmystwyth, Rhandirmwyn and my old home of Llanddewi Brefi, as well as dozens of outlying farms and cottages. It was from these rural outposts that sheep and cattle were once driven over the uplands to markets in England. It is a stunning part of the world that offers great value for money in a raw and visceral landscape that I think provides for one of the few tangible old-school rural lifestyles in Britain, one that's as governed by the weather as it is by the mountains themselves.

The raw beauty of the landscape of Afon Claerwen. It's quite possible to walk its hills and valleys all day and not see another soul.

West Wales

A search for the good life was what drew one lucky couple to Pembrokeshire, but in the end the charms of Carmarthenshire proved irresistible.

Caught on camera: the moment I revealed the price of this property to both Steve and Di changed everything. Just a few weeks later they were moving in.

In June 2017 I met up with Steve and Di from Eastleigh in Hampshire. Steve had just retired from his job as an HGV driver and Di was following suit from her job as a chef. For years Di had been a passionate horse-rider and carriage driver, and owned two ponies, which she'd always stabled away from home. But with Eastleigh becoming busier and more developed they felt it was time to make the jump while they still could, to find a rural life that would be quieter and allow them to have their horses at home. This was clearly an exciting move, but also a huge emotional wrench; Steve had been born in their current home and despite his 62 years had never bought another.

This whole adventure would broker a series of firsts for both of them.

They chose Pembrokeshire in south-west Wales as the focus for their search. They wanted a detached house with two or three bedrooms, a large kitchen-diner and around 3 acres not just for the ponies but also for some pigs and possibly chickens, and they were toying with the idea of a holiday let if the right opportunity arose. They were fortunate to have a budget of £450,000 but knew that even in the western wilds of Wales they might struggle.

Blessed with scorching weather we set about viewing two really good properties that offered everything they

were after. The first was a recent renovation and much extended four-bedroom house that came with 7 acres for £425,000, while the second, equally priced farmhouse came with only 5 acres but had plenty of outbuildings with holiday let potential if converted.

However, it was our mystery house that carried them both away, as well it might. Over the border into Carmarthenshire we travelled towards my old haunt on the edge of the Cambrian Mountains to find a beautifully renovated and extended stone cottage with 8 acres and breathtaking views.

Within seven weeks of filming they had bought it and moved in. Three months afterwards we all met up to see how they were getting on and they could not have been happier. For Steve, his old life in Eastleigh is a distant memory; the sense of space and peace that surrounds their new home has given him a new lease of life as a hobby farmer. Di is delighted that her ponies are outside the kitchen window, and they have already taken on two rare breed Large White pigs to go with the flock of rescued battery hens that now supply them with eggs for Steve's cake baking hobby.

If not purely the good life, they are as close to it as most of us would want to be – and they achieved it for a final price of £430,000. It's given them a gorgeous home with far-reaching views and a beautiful 8 acres; but perhaps more importantly they have invested in a new life. Can you really put a price on that?

Right above: The interior of this house was typical of many historic properties in the area, offering cosy charm with the character and texture that only ancient stone walls can bring.

Right: Sympathetically extended and improved over many years, the property's most recent period of renovation produced a stunning proposition that sold itself. Although not initially in the right place, it was certainly the right price.

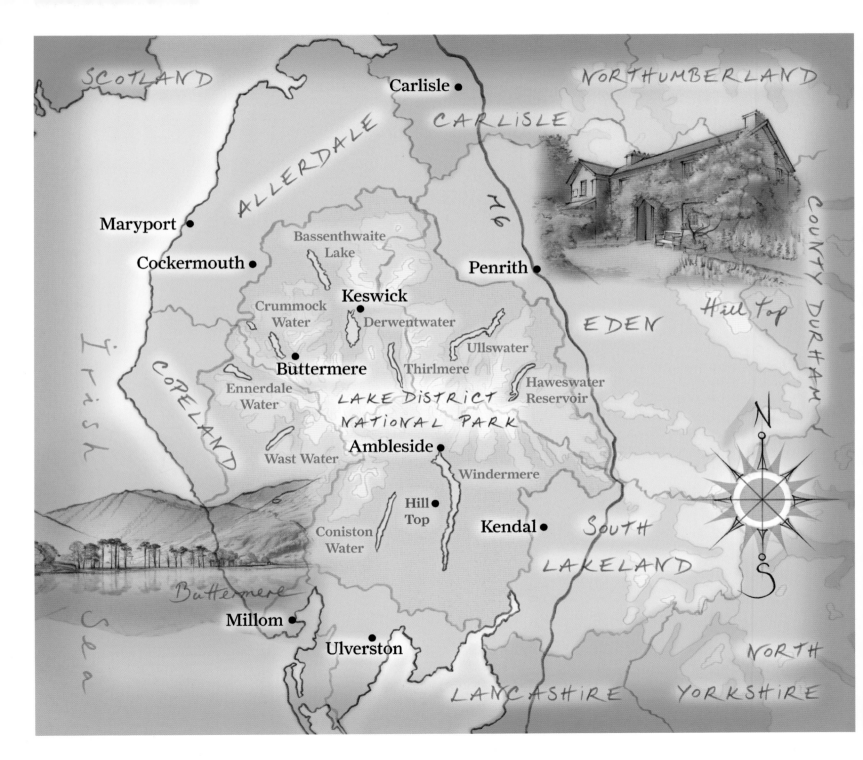

SCOTLAND

NORTHUMBERLAND

Carlisle •

CARLISLE

ALLERDALE

M6

Maryport •

Bassenthwaite
Lake

Penrith •

EDEN

Cockermouth •

Hill Top

Keswick
•

Crummock
Water

Derwentwater

Irish

Buttermere

Ullswater

COPELAND

Ennerdale
Water

Thirlmere

Haweswater
Reservoir

LAKE DISTRICT

NATIONAL PARK

Wast Water

Ambleside •

N

Windermere

Hill
Top •

Coniston
Water

Kendal •

SOUTH

LAKELAND

S

Buttermere

Sea

Millom •

NORTH

Ulverston •

LANCASHIRE

YORKSHIRE

COUNTY DURHAM

The Lake District

I defy anyone who's been to the Lake District not to be moved by the majesty of the landscape. Five hundred million years of geological evolution have resulted in breathtaking mountains, ridges, valleys and, of course, lakes. Valleys radiate out from a 'hub' at Dunmail Raise accommodating the 14 lakes and tarns that give the area its name.

The dramatic views, painted with nature's beautiful colour palate, are a powerful draw, with most of us forgiving the changing and unpredictable weather for which the area is also known. No wonder it has long been a favourite haunt of artists and writers. This is a timeless landscape with a long history; from the prehistoric stone circle at Castlerigg to the ancient Neolithic axe factories high up on Great Langdale.

Thousands of miles of stone walls drape across the heights and valleys like lace, while numerous stone-built cottages, farmhouses and great Victorian villas overlook some of the finest lakeside views you will find. Whatever your reasons for coming here you'll be in good company if you decide it's where you want to live.

The writer Alfred Wainwright famously mapped hundreds of walking routes that cover the entire district, and his books continue to inspire many of the estimated 16 million visitors a year the region attracts.

Waterhead Cottages on the Monk Coniston Estate.

Artists' paradise

William Wordsworth grew up here, and his 1820 work, *Guide through the District of the Lakes*, helped establish the region as a tourist destination. You can visit the house in Cockermouth in which he was born in 1770, now run by the National Trust. The desk where he carved his name is also preserved at his school in Hawkshead.

J. M. W. Turner travelled to the Lakes to visit his friend and patron, the 3rd Earl of Egremont, and, inspired by the scenery, he captured it on canvas leading to a new appreciation of landscape art.

Beatrix Potter famously made the Lakes her home and championed the region and its distinctive Herdwick Sheep that still dominate the landscape. The National Trust are custodians of her seventeenth-century farmhouse, Hill Top, and it is open for visits during the summer months.

It was with the proceeds of her first book, *The Tale of Peter Rabbit* that Beatrix Potter bought Hill Top in 1905, and it was here that many of her most memorable characters were subsequently brought to life, depicted in her inimitable style and surrounded by many objects still on display within. Her love of the Lake District, its customs, history and people have long endeared her to locals and visitors alike, while keen-eyed architectural pilgrims can revel in a traditional Cumbrian upland farmhouse that has been beautifully preserved and presented, just as Beatrix herself had wished.

It was here too that graphite was first discovered back in the sixteenth century, becoming so valuable that it gave rise to illicit mining and trade that spawned the phrase 'Black Market'. Today that legacy is maintained by Derwent Graphics, the modern incarnation of Cumberland Pencils, which still make millions of them every year, just as they have since 1832. There is a small museum in Keswick that charts the company's history and is well worth a visit.

Sunset over Crummock Water; the rosy glow in the sky is reflected in the shimmering surface of the lake. This is a view that inspired J. M. W. Turner.

Below: The vegetable garden at Hill Top, now maintained by the National Trust. A wooden beehive sits in the bee bole, exactly as it did in Beatrix's time, and tools are arranged among the vegetables in homage to Mr McGregor.

Right: A view onto the landing from a bedroom at Hill Top.

It will come as no surprise that properties within the boundaries of the National Park, which is now also a UNESCO World Heritage site, will come at a premium. On average, house prices in National Parks are around 50 per cent higher than those in the surrounding county. In the case of the Lakes, this premium is a whopping 100 per cent, so it is worth considering the options beyond its borders. Towns like Millom, Cockermouth and Penrith all sit just outside the Park and are worth exploring for access to all the Lakes have to offer but without the property premium you will find inside the Park. The western Lakes, although less accessible, may also give you better value than the more popular central districts.

I've long felt two of the defining characteristics of the Lake District are the ever changing hues of purple that take your eye into the distance, and the crisp reflections that the mountains can conjure whatever the weather. This winter morning across Derwent Water is a perfect example.

Part of the charm of the Lake District is the fact that its narrow lanes and steep climbs force a much slower pace on both visitors and locals alike – nowhere is quick to get to, but once you are there the landscape rewards you time and again. Since the Victorians began the fashion of holidaying here, the main hubs around Keswick and Windermere have catered for a tourist industry that thrives in some grand hotels and numerous holiday lets and cottages.

Framed by the distant outline of the mountains beyond, this image of the great Neolithic Stone Circle at Castlerigg represents, for many, the ancient spirit of the Lake District landscape. Now in the care of the National Trust and visited by thousands of people every year, it has been studied and reinterpreted many times over the last 300 years. Almost certainly arranged as a calendar to both reflect and respect lunar and solar events, since it was built around 3200 BC it has cast its own spell over the surrounding fells, and remains one of the most important monuments of its kind in the world.

Above: Bridge House at Ambleside may appear precarious, but it has been admired for centuries.

Left: The third largest of the region's lakes, Coniston Water has been popular with writers and artists for generations. It was here that Arthur Ransome set many of the tales from *Swallows and Amazons*, and where too the tranquil waters were troubled by numerous attempts to beat the world water speed record. In 1939 Sir Malcolm Campbell reached just over 141mph, while nearly 30 years later his son Donald lost his life when his craft *Bluebird* crashed at over 320mph. In 2001 the wreck was finally retrieved from the bottom of the lake, and has since undergone a fascinating reconstruction.

FOOTPATHS

Over thousands of years, the web of footpaths and other minor rights of way that criss-cross the UK have extended to a staggering 150,000 miles. This extraordinary network of ancient routes provides unique public access to enormous swathes of countryside. Their legal standing has been enshrined since the Second World War in various statutes; the 1949 National Parks and Access to the Countryside Act; and the more recent Town and Country Planning Act of 1990. The former not only established the National Parks, it also defined *Areas of Outstanding Natural Beauty*, as well as creating most of the nation's long-distance so-called *Continuous* Paths, which flow in or around our National Parks, such as the Pembrokeshire Coastal Path, the North and South Downs Way, the Pennine Way, the Cleveland Way, Offa's Dyke Path and the Ridgeway Path.

There are many more celebrated examples that have become important trails, drawing together key points of the landscape and regional histories, the majority evolved from ancient and long-established routeways.

Drovers' roads that helped get livestock to market, old Roman roads that have now been abandoned, mass or church paths that linked places of worship over which coffins might have been carried (corpse roads), tow paths alongside canals, pilgrim paths connecting key monastic sites or sunken roads that may trace their origins back into prehistory, they all have a story to tell and are fascinating rights of way open to us all.

These days, rights of way are recorded upon what is known as the *Definitive Map*. It is a document updated and held by the local authority, either council or National Park where relevant, and it details where each path runs. You'll also find each parish will have a local volunteer footpaths officer whose job it is to oversee their maintenance, regularly checking for obstructions or decay.

If you are thinking of buying a property that is crossed by a footpath, it's important to understand that it is virtually impossible to remove it,

although it may be possible to divert it slightly if you can create an alternative but non-permanent *permissive* route that is of increased benefit to the user. However, the system is weighted to favour the right of way, as are the costs of applying to have it permanently changed or blocked, which can easily run into thousands of pounds. Few applications to permanently remove a footpath are ever successful. In short, if you aren't happy with a footpath through your proposed property then don't buy it. However, if like me, your new home has one and you are prepared to take it on, then go ahead, and enjoy the cheery waves of walkers as they wander through.

Enabling travellers to get over obstacles in the way of a footpath is the job of the humble stile. They come in various forms depending on the obstacle they are designed to deal with, and whereabouts in the country you are, but essentially they all do the same job; they maintain access to the route while keeping fences and walls intact and livestock secure.

Architecturally, the geology of the Lakes has defined the style of many properties on offer. Stone, quarried or gathered locally, has been commonly used for the walls of the most picturesque cottages and farms, built in the heart of the National Park, while further out, granite, limestone and red sandstone have all been used in a kaleidoscope of buildings.

Right: View across the kitchen garden to the back of Wordsworth House, Cockermouth, Cumbria, the birthplace and childhood home of the poet.

Below: Herdwick sheep, Borrowdale, Cumbria.

Opposite: A view of Hill Top, Cumbria, Beatrix Potter's own Escape to the Country. It now attracts thousands of visitors every year.

Alternative location to the Lake District

Powys

One hurdle when planning a move to the Lake District can be distance from family and friends, particularly if you are relocating from the south. From London, it's a good five- to six-hour drive, although an efficient three-hour train ride will get you from London to Penrith, so if you fancy a similar feel, with mountains, lakes and accessibility, Powys in Wales is a good option. Only three hours by car away from the capital and even closer to Birmingham and Manchester, Powys is home to the Brecon Beacons and, as Wales's largest county, it runs right up to Snowdonia. Prices are attractive, and for anyone wanting lots of property with land and outbuildings, yet within striking distance of the rest of the central belt and the capital, it is certainly worth considering. Brecon itself, Crickhowell, Builth Wells and Rhayader would be my starting points for a search.

Above: The Canal Dock in Brecon was once a hive of commercial activity. Like most canals today it's hub for a thriving tourist scene.

Left: The highest peaks of the Brecon Beacons, Pen y Fan and Corn Du, seen to the north-west from Mynydd Illtud Common.

Stornoway

N
S

Isle of
Skye

Glen
Affric

Inverness

Crathes Castle

Great
Glen Way

Cairngorms
National Park

Aberdeen

Crathes Castle

Fort
William

Ben Nevis

Ardnamurchan

Tobermory

Glen Coe

Dundee

Isle of
Mull

Loch Lomond
& The Trossachs
National Park

North
Sea

Stirling

Edinburgh

Linlithgow

Glasgow

Isle of
Arran

SCOTLAND

Kelso

Melrose

Northumberland
National Park

Ben Nevis

Galloway
Forest Park

IRELAND

ENGLAND

Kircudbright

Scotland

The Borders, Highlands and Islands

Scotland is a huge country, so huge in fact that I defy anyone to have explored every corner. While I too have only just scratched the surface of what Scotland has to offer, a decade of house hunting here has shown it to be a diverse and beautiful nation. The vibrant cities of Glasgow to the west and Edinburgh to the east are natural starting points for any exploratory adventure, from where you can travel south to the Scottish Borders with their rolling lowlands and chequered political, military and economic history, and north to the Highlands and Islands.

The Scottish Borders are popular with many house hunters because they combine the magic ingredients of affordability with great countryside and, relatively speaking, good connectivity to the south. Unlike the drama of the Highlands, the Lowlands are more rolling and easier to get around. As well as finding plenty of houses with many appealing views, you'll also have the chance to pick from a host of pretty market towns, with Kelso being chief among them. Regarded by many as a jewel in Scotland's architectural crown, this

The sight of a roaring fire in an historic highland property takes some beating.

ancient place began life in the early twelfth century when Kelso Abbey was founded. Since then it has developed into a beautiful town, distinctive in having cobbled streets and a central square, which perhaps feels more continental-European than Scottish.

The Highlands, with their vast lochs are a stunning upland wilderness that's home to many rare species of wildlife, including a handful of the sadly almost extinct native wildcat. The infamous Highland Clearances of the eighteenth and nineteenth centuries, which saw thousands of tenants evicted from their farms and smallholdings, left much of the landscape empty of the settlements that you might see in other upland areas of the UK. Not surprisingly in a huge, now underpopulated, region, house hunting here takes time; getting from A to B is rarely a quick process, a fact that reflects the general pace of life in the region, something that is a welcome and important factor for those who come here looking to get away from it all.

If you really do crave isolation, then Scotland could well be for you. However, with four international airports (Aberdeen, Edinburgh, Glasgow and Glasgow Prestwick) and many more regional airports, as well as some good rail links, connecting to the rest of the UK, and world, is easier now than it's ever been.

My favourite spots are the coast near Fort William; including the famous landmarks of Glen Coe and Ben Nevis, and the area south and west of Inverness, which I've been lucky enough to spend some time in. Glen Affric, less well known than its neighbouring Glen Coe, is enchanting and will leave you feeling as far away from the hustle and bustle as is possible.

Scotland also boasts some outstanding property, from huge baronial estates that encompass thousands of acres of the sort made famous in series such as *Monarch of the Glen*, to the ubiquitous and enchanting single-storey whitewashed crofts that still pepper the upland landscape. Historically, property prices have been far more attractive than elsewhere in the UK because of the lack of large industrial centres and the isolated nature of settlements and outlying properties. There is a good range of options for most budgets, and we have often gone property shopping with £250,000 or less with great results. A budget that might struggle to get you a four-bedroom house in west London, could buy you a small country estate complete with river fishing rights in parts of Scotland.

So vast is the Scottish countryside and coastline that it is worth considering the advantages of life in one of its many market towns or coastal centres. The vast Scottish landscape is still very accessible, but you will have all the amenities and sense of community you might be after. For example, Kelso or Melrose in the southern Borders, Kirkcudbright overlooking the River Dee, Tobermory on Mull, and Linlithgow in between Stirling and Edinburgh are options that won't disappoint. If you have need of regular medical attention, or fear you may do in the future, it is certainly worth thinking about life in or near a settlement that can help you; few parts of the UK offer such a genuine sense of splendid isolation as rural Scotland, but it's worth remembering that a trip to a hospital A&E department could be a couple of hours away.

Right: Despite their somewhat fierce appearance, Highland cattle are generally known to have a good temperament, although as with all livestock they should be treated with due care, not least when they have their young nearby as here in Glen Coe.

Below: Fort William and Loch Linnhe.

Left: Ardnamurchan. This peninsula has the distinction of being the most westerly in the British Isles and exudes an air of remote splendour whatever the weather. If you are thinking of getting away from it all, then Scotland's north-west coast is one part of the British Isles that genuinely delivers the dream.

Below: Crathes Castle (National Trust for Scotland), started in 1553, is a fine example of Scottish baronial architecture. While many tower houses stand as romantic ruins that betray their turbulent past, many more have survived intact or have been renovated into spectacular homes.

Opposite: When seen from above, the Great Glen that runs diagonally from the Moray Firth at Inverness down to Fort William on the west coast effectively cuts Scotland in two. The small highland roads on either side offer some of the most memorable views in Britain, with surprisingly affordable property that makes the best of this enormous landscape.

ARRAN – ISLAND LIFE

For many years, I hoped that we'd have the chance to *Escape to the Country* on the Isle of Arran. I first visited the island as a teenager, so when the chance arose in the spring of 2018 to help a couple who'd long dreamed of moving there, I jumped at it. With a modest budget of £250,000 we explored the island from top to bottom. It soon cast its magic spell over us all, and proved the point that if you are prepared to move almost anywhere, great property within a lively community and stunning setting is very achievable. What's more there is something wholly unique about island life, something I've experienced on Anglesey, off the north Welsh coast. Being surrounded by the sea, the elements combine to create a climate that is specific to where you live, somehow creating a sense of unity within the community. House prices are often lower than in mainland coastal hotspots such as Cornwall or the channel coast, meaning that if a coastal life is for you, house hunting on an island like this can deliver exactly what you are looking for without costing the earth.

Opposite: Arran's unspoilt landscape offers coastal seclusion and unbeatable views at an affordable price compared with more southerly hotspots like Cornwall – provided island, highland life is for you.

Left: Sheep graze in the shadow of an old stone barn on remote Machrie Moor.

Below: The bridge at Catacol on the north-west side of the island.

151

Crofts in the Highlands and Islands

Specific to Scotland's Highlands and Islands is a type of smallholding known as a croft. The croft refers to a parcel of land – usually between 5 and 12 acres – and has traditionally been occupied by tenants who've often enjoyed further access to common grazing nearby. The house, should the land have had one, was built by the crofter, and tended to be low, single-storey, stone-built affairs with thatched roofs. Crofting remains a huge part of the life and economy of the Highlands, and can offer the prospect of smallholding in some of the most captivating and demanding landscapes Britain has to offer.

The croft itself was a response to the tragedy of the Highland Clearances, but today the rights of the tenant crofter have been enshrined in several Acts passed by the Scottish Parliament, a process that began in the late nineteenth century. Among other factors, recent changes to the 1973 Act have made it much easier for crofters to buy their land should they wish, while crofters now enjoy far greater security of tenure. Crofts do occasionally come up for sale on the open market, while a list of available crofts to tenant is available from two main sources: the Crofters Register and the Register of Crofts. Tenants are required to live no further than 20 miles from their croft – but you can have more than one. Many crofters however have bought their titles and become owner-occupiers, while grants have been available to help with building newer buildings on croft land.

Splendid isolation. For many, this image of a croft dwarfed by the majesty of the mountains around Glen Coe is the ultimate escape.

Today there are an estimated 19,000 crofts in Scotland which together make a significant contribution to the rural economy. They are home to 33,000 families, 10 per cent of the Highlands and Islands population, and they produce 20 per cent of Scotland's beef stock and 45 per cent of the nation's breeding ewes, some 1.5 million of them.

The architecture of the traditional croft was stone, with a thatch, slate or possibly peat roof, with small windows and doors to keep the biting wind and weather at bay. While many examples of these small historic properties still exist, a growing number of new-builds are springing up in the Highlands where these architectural traditions are being rethought. New materials for wall coverings such as tin and timber, and the greater use of thermally efficient glass, removing the need to make windows small, makes the best of some amazing views. It is easy to forget when surrounded by the majesty of the Highland landscape that it's been founded on change throughout its history. These new and eye-catching buildings are as at home in the hills and on loch-sides as any others, and are redefining what Highland life is like. Both sensational in looks and efficient to run, they have successfully borrowed from the shape of things past while assuredly looking to the future.

Opposite, clockwise from bottom left: Today's architects, such as those at R.House based on the Isle of Skye, are rethinking the traditional croft. This one at Grealin combines the stonework of an original ruined croft with their own signature mix of timber, zinc and windows that make the best of its stunning aspect and views. It is in stark contrast to the traditional lines of Gearrannan Blackhouse Village, a crofting township on the Isle of Lewis in the Outer Hebrides, and a classic example at Malacleit on North Uist.

Above: I defy anyone not to be inspired by a lifestyle shaped by the surrounding highlands and the unique weather they can conjure.

Argyll & Bute

For this couple a move from the flatlands of Lincolnshire to the rugged drama of the Highlands was one way to ensure that the next chapter in their lives was unlike anything that had gone before.

Jonnie with Steve and Rebecca. The highland landscape and property market always makes for an inspiring house hunt regardless of the budget.

For Rebecca and Steve, the difference in the life they swapped from the flatlands around Brigg in Lincolnshire to one in the coastal highlands of Argyll & Bute could not have been more marked. Steve was running his own renewable energy business and Rebecca was thinking about retiring, but they had an idea that the Scottish Highlands would offer them the sort of extreme shift of lifestyle they sought, to ring the changes from one chapter of their lives to another.

Armed with a budget of £350,000, in the spring of 2015 they joined Jonnie Irwin for a Highland odyssey that would have far-reaching results. They were clear they wanted to be close to

the coast, they wanted three bedrooms and, if possible, an open-plan layout. The prospect of a project was clearly of interest and Steve was keen to bring his expertise in renewable energy systems to a new home that would use similar technologies to those they had already employed in their current property in Lincolnshire. They were also bringing their two dogs with them so wanted easy access to the countryside, and were actively seeking a sense of being remote, an easy fix in this stunning part of the world.

Jonnie set about showing them three properties, all of which were under budget, giving them plenty to consider, not least the striking sea views across to

the Isle of Arran at his second property. Yet after much deliberation it was the first one they saw that they eventually bought. In 2017, I had the chance to catch up with them as they began to really settle into their new life in the Highlands and celebrate Rebecca's recent retirement.

It was obvious that their new home was a perfect fit. Built around 1850 it had undergone a crisp and thoughtful renovation that gave them the open-plan layout they were after. It also meant that there was still plenty of scope to improve the property's green footprint. They plan to install a more eco-friendly heating system and open up the living room with a sweep of sun-catching bifold doors that will make the best of the views to the rear over the surrounding mountains, a fair trade given they had originally wanted sea views. That said, they are just a short distance from the banks of neighbouring Loch Eck and a few miles from the coast at Dunoon. Originally on the market for £315,000 they eventually bought it for £295,000, leaving plenty left over to make the changes they wanted to.

Right: This move proved that if you value affordable property surrounded by breathtaking scenery, Scotland won't disappoint.

Below: Holy Loch was home to US nuclear submarines during the Cold War; today, the shores near Dunoon are once again tranquil, set against a highland backdrop.

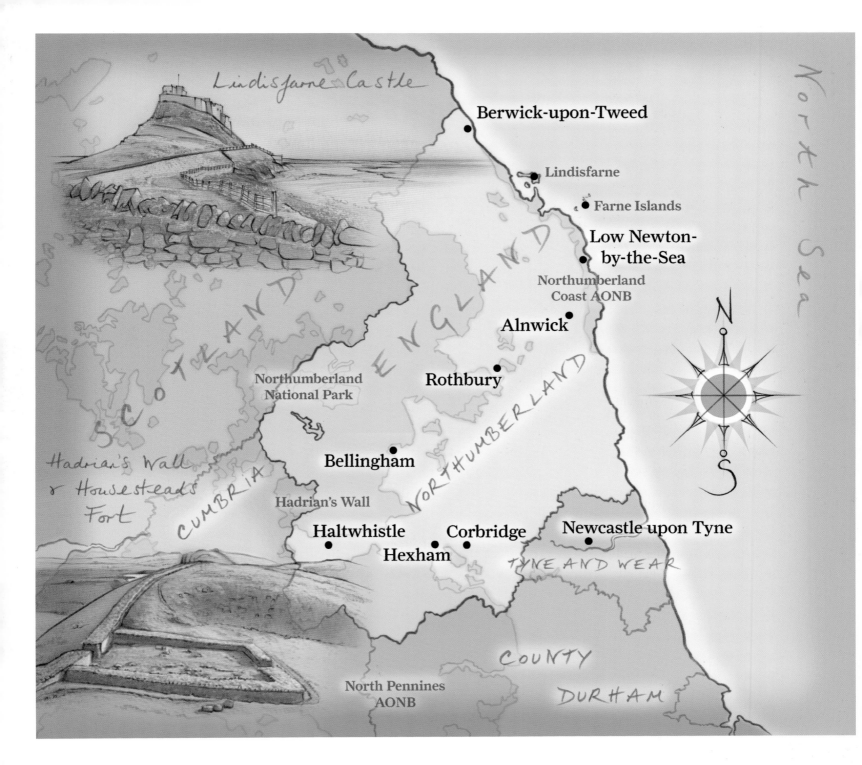

Lindisfarne Castle

Berwick-upon-Tweed

Lindisfarne

Farne Islands

Low Newton-
by-the-Sea

Northumberland
Coast AONB

Alnwick

ENGLAND

SCOTLAND

Northumberland
National Park

Rothbury

NORTHUMBERLAND

Bellingham

Hadrian's Wall
& Housesteads
Fort

Hadrian's Wall

CUMBRIA

Haltwhistle

Hexham

Corbridge

Newcastle upon Tyne

TYNE AND WEAR

North Pennines
AONB

COUNTY

DURHAM

North Sea

N

S

The North East

The North East is an area I fell in love with over 20 years ago when I was lucky enough to spend some time studying in the area. Since then, every visit has been a treat. I recall my first trip to Hadrian's Wall as an archaeologist. This extraordinary feature of the landscape stretches out between two seas, cutting the country in half. The landscape either side of it is scattered with pretty towns and villages such as Hexham and Corbridge that owe their origins to the Roman legions that first ventured northwards and then stopped to consolidate the edge of the Empire.

Like many border counties, Northumberland has been shaped by conflict. It was on the island of Lindisfarne that Christianity gained an early foothold and suffered at the hands of the Vikings. Later medieval coastal fortresses such as Warkworth and Dunstanburgh remain, as powerful symbols of the region's military past, but thankfully these days it is a far more peaceful place.

It is the rich history here that makes this landscape exciting, and it's palpable. From the prehistoric hillforts of the Cheviot Hills, through its extensive Roman remains, the Viking legacy, and the lasting influence of Norman conquests and endless border quarrels throughout the centuries, the story of Northumberland is in many ways a barometer of the fortunes

The Bunkhouse at Cragside, Northumberland, was created from two converted Victorian workers' cottages.

of the UK as a whole. It's a county packed with sights to see. It should come as no surprise then that it was voted as the best holiday destination in the UK for 2018, a significant achievement when you look at the competition.

Northumberland's architecture spans everything from medieval tower houses to stone-built upland cottages, manor houses to fishermen's cottages on the coast. The Georgian and Victorian periods have also left their mark in the terraces and Neo-classical public buildings that line the streets of significant market towns like Berwick-upon-Tweed, but it is the local stone that really defines the property market here, and embeds the region's finest homes within its striking and often unforgiving landscape.

In terms of Northumberland's rural highlights, many are encompassed by the Northumberland National Park, the most northerly in England. Comprising huge upland moors, many of which now form part of the military training area of Otterburn, it also includes the rolling Cheviot Hills, a popular haunt for walkers, not least those that frequent the section of the Pennine Way that connects Northumberland with Cumbria to the west, and Scotland to the north. The southern end of the Park also takes in the central section of Hadrian's Wall, around the impressive remains of the huge legionary fortress at Housesteads.

The Park also includes the Border Forest, created by the Forestry Commission in 1926, following the First World War, and the largest man-made forest in Europe. At its heart is the huge body of Kielder Water, itself the largest man-made lake in northern Europe, both of which are easily reached from the charming market town of Bellingham.

The Kielder Observatory overlooking Kielder Water and Forest Park, Northumberland. The area is famed for having the darkest night skies in England, and since the observatory opened in 2008, it has hosted hundreds of events and allowed thousands of people to experience the wonders of space.

Premium Northumberland

When it comes to property, the urban magnet of Newcastle upon Tyne can, unsurprisingly, add a premium to homes that might be considered a commutable distance away, but in general Northumberland does offer pretty good value for money.

As our working patterns become increasingly flexible and the pace of entrepreneurial start-ups continues, options for living more remotely, away from major UK conurbations, increase. Having these options vastly improves the choices of where to make your home and Northumberland is well worth considering.

Corbridge

When you walk through the pretty honey-coloured stone streets and peruse its fine array of independent shops you'd be forgiven for forgetting that Corbridge was once the most northerly town in the Roman Empire. On the outskirts of the current settlement the remains of the Roman town that began life as a fort back in AD 85 – some 37 years before Hadrian set about building his great wall – are easily explored. Over many centuries, the successive bridges that have crossed the River Tyne here have made Corbridge strategically significant, but today its often-turbulent borderland past is confined to history and it is now one of the most popular of Northumberland's towns to visit and live in, helped in large part by the train service to Newcastle.

Above: The historic town of Corbridge, known as Corstopitum by the Romans, was built to supply troops manning Hadrian's Wall. The site of the Roman settlement has been excavated and can be viewed just north of the modern town. The Roman town survived into the fifth century, and features include shops, townhouses and military barracks.

Opposite: The first bridge across the River Tyne at Corbridge was built in the thirteenth century. The medieval bridge fell into disrepair and was finally replaced in 1674 by the one we see today. This was the only bridge on the Tyne to survive the devastating floods of 1771.

Harthope Valley. The great eighteenth-century writers Daniel Defoe and Sir Walter Scott both reportedly walked this remote valley and rolling uplands unfettered by towns or villages. With a similar feel to the Cambrian Mountains of Mid Wales, isolated farms and cottages are scattered over a landscape that provides ready access to the Cheviot Hills.

Above: Located in the heart of Coquetdale, Rothbury is the perfect jumping-off point for forays into the National Park and the nearby Simonside Hills. Pretty sandstone architecture also characterises this settlement, which has graced the banks of the River Coquet since it came to prominence in the thirteenth century.

Right: Considered by many to be one of the prettiest of Northumberland's coastal villages, Low Newton is now largely in the care of the National Trust; its central square and low cottages are a step back into the eighteenth century. The coastal walk that connects Low Newton to Dunstanburgh Castle has been rated as one of the top 10 walks in the UK in recent years, confirming that the unique beauty of this stretch of coastline makes it a destination in its own right.

Farne Islands – a remote treat

A few years ago, I had the chance to visit this tiny, uninhabited archipelago of 14 islands off the north-east coast of England. I was doing a Radio 4 interview with a unique group of conservationists who spend nine months of the year on the main island. Charged with monitoring the wildlife, their particular interest was in the pupping rate of one of the largest colonies of Atlantic grey seals in Britain, an event they record every year. Living in the old lighthouse-keeper's cottage this hardy and committed bunch lived a life I came to envy, surrounded by the volatile North Sea, the weather and the seals. When it comes to spending time immersed in your surroundings, I've not seen anything to beat it.

When I first came to Northumberland it was to work on the building of a small wind farm in the coastal town of Blyth in the early 1990s. I returned as a postgraduate student at Durham University, and since then I've been captivated by the landscapes, coastlines, architecture and warmth of the people I've met. I've heard talk of high rainfall and cold north-easterly winds putting prospective buyers off, but to heed such gossip is to miss out on the chance to live in one of the great historic counties of Britain, one that while savouring its past is always looking towards the future. From the heights of the Cheviots to Newcastle's cool quayside bars, my advice is not to write Northumberland off until you've seen it for yourself. I doubt you'll want to leave.

Left: This view of the spectacular remains of Dunstanburgh Castle from the coast at Craster appears almost Arthurian. It will come as no surprise that this is a region rich in folklore, myth and legend.

Right: Each year, puffins return to the Farne Islands to breed, generally between April and late July, with the peak breeding season in May and June. For the rest of the year, the birds fly out to sea, overwintering on the water, only returning to land when it is time to breed once again.

It's sometimes easy to forget that these now humble remains of Hadrian's Wall once marked the edge of the greatest empire the world had ever known, one that stretched from the North East to the Middle East.

This stone cottage at Once Brewed has stood in the shadow of Hadrian's Wall for at least 200 years.

Upland stone farms and cottages

There is a hardy theme that runs through both the people and the buildings that occupy our uplands. Historically, they offered the prospect of cheaper land upon which to farm and build, provided materials were readily available, and even today it takes a certain kind of determined soul to take on the often very unique challenges of upland life. Yet, by definition, properties in these areas tend to come with wonderful views, while the odds are that the building itself will have been well built from substantial local stone. What rooms may lack in size, they will often more than make up for in cosy comforts, allowing you to settle down against the worst of the weather.

Above: The exterior of Cherryburn, the ground floor being a museum and the upper floor the administrator's residence. Cherryburn is the birthplace of artist and naturalist Thomas Bewick. Bewick was a wood engraver and naturalist who revolutionised print art in Georgian England. Set in a tranquil garden with views across the Tyne Valley, the house is surrounded by the natural world that inspired his work.

Left: This eighteenth-century whitewashed stone cottage next to Wylam Waggonway on the south bank of the River Tyne was once the home of rail pioneer George Stephenson.

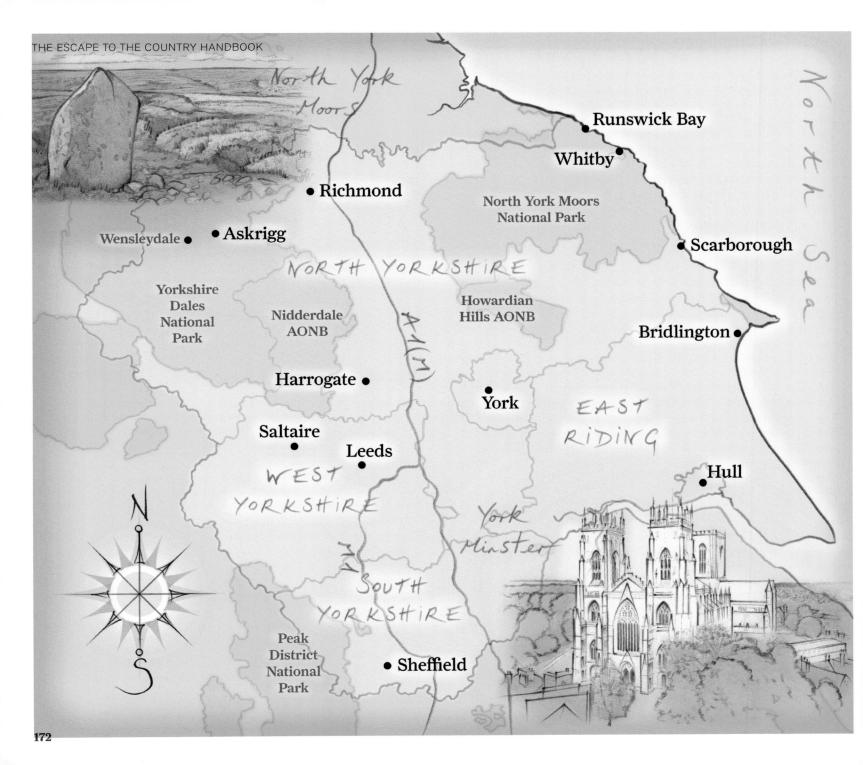

North York
Moors

Runswick Bay

Whitby

North York Moors
National Park

Richmond

Wensleydale • • Askrigg

NORTH YORKSHIRE

Scarborough

Yorkshire
Dales
National
Park

Nidderdale
AONB

Howardian
Hills AONB

Bridlington •

A1(M)

Harrogate •

York •

EAST
RIDING

Saltaire
•

Leeds
•

Hull •

WEST

YORKSHIRE

York
Minster

SOUTH

YORKSHIRE

Peak
District
National
Park

• Sheffield

North Sea

North Sea

N

S

Yorkshire

Few locals are as proud of their roots as those from Yorkshire, which they describe as 'God's own county'. Blessed with some of the most beautiful countryside Britain has to offer as well as some stunning coastline, Yorkshire also comes with one of the most popular city break destinations, in York itself. Tracing its history right back to the Romans, the streets of this former Viking stronghold are now lined with independent shops and overlooked by the majesty of both York Minster and its castle, while the River Ouse that meanders through it gives it the atmosphere of a timeless European city.

As befits such a huge county, some of Yorkshire's most prized landscapes have been drawn together within its three National Parks: the Yorkshire Dales, the North York Moors and a large swathe of the Peak District National Park, while Areas of Outstanding Natural Beauty also abound.

Yorkshire's cultural identity stretches way beyond its borders, and has touched many parts of the world through tea and cricket, among many other things. Yorkshire treasures include actors Dame Judi Dench, Michael Palin, Ben Kingsley, Sean Bean and Brian Blessed, while artists David Hockney and Henry Moore have long championed its heritage. Some of the country's greatest writers were born in Yorkshire, not least the Brontë sisters, J. B. Priestley and Alan

This pretty village terrace is typical of many in the Yorkshire Dales.

The viaduct at Knaresborough, just 10 minutes by train from Harrogate, spans the River Nidd in dramatic style, while still carrying the railway. Harrogate itself is often voted as one of the best places to live, not just in Yorkshire, but in the UK as a whole.

Bennett. Thomas Chippendale's name is synonymous with furnishing the homes of the rich and famous from the eighteenth century. Industrialist Titus Salt led a revolution in the design and operation of textile milling, and left a legacy in the great monument to compassionate capitalism he created in the 1850s at Saltaire or Salts Mill near Bradford. Setting the standard for many model villages since, it incorporated a hospital, a bath house and alms-houses for retired employees. At the time it was built, the mill was the largest building of its kind in the world and has more recently been the focus of an ambitious restoration project.

Yorkshire people have a creative ambition and a healthy regard for hard work which has since characterised much of the folklore that surrounds the county. It is by far Britain's biggest county and combines the four distinct districts of North, South and East Yorkshire as well as the West Riding. During the Wars of the Roses in the fifteenth century, where Richard III struggled for supremacy, the White Rose of Yorkshire was pitted against the Red Rose of neighbouring Lancashire. The rivalry between the houses of York and Lancaster is now thankfully much friendlier and usually confined to the cricket pitch.

Architecturally the upland farmsteads and nucleated villages of the Dales and North York moors appear to have risen from the rocky landscape itself. Worn by centuries of wind and rain the dry-stone walls and field barns for which areas like Swaledale are famous, offer a timeless style. Larger rectories, manors and stately homes sit side by side with cottages, chapels and converted mills, yet they are linked by the colour and texture of the stone that has been used to build them, and centuries of history that surrounds them.

Right above: If you are thinking of a move to North Yorkshire, but still want the benefits of living in a vibrant town with easy access to great countryside, the historic market town of Richmond could well be the answer. Its strategic position overlooking the River Swale has been recognised since it was founded back in 1071. The impressive castle overlooks one of the biggest market squares in Britain, the commercial success of which has ensured the town is bursting with a wealth of period property too, not least the many Georgian houses that line its streets. What's more, Richmond shares its name with a further 57 towns around the world, but as the locals here will proudly tell you, North Yorkshire's was the first.

Right below: Yorkshire's harsh winter weather demands a lot from the livestock that grazes its fells and dales. The Swaledale sheep that cover the landscape have been bred over the years to cope with the tough upland environment without the need for much shelter. Hardy and self-reliant, they are easily recognised thanks to their characteristic off-white fleece, black and white faces and distinctive curled horns. Long synonymous with the region, the breed today is a proud symbol of the Yorkshire Dales.

Opposite: One of the most distinctive features of the Dales is the high number of stone field barns or laithes. Within the boundaries of the Yorkshire Dales National Park, an estimated 4,000 survive. Unlike most other farm buildings, the field barn was sited away from the main farmstead, and within the web of enclosed field boundaries created from the eighteenth century onwards. Built originally for overwintering cattle and storing feed close to remote pastures, modern farming techniques have now left many redundant, while their survival as important architectural features of the Dales is now increasingly recognised by local authorities keen to see them maintained, with some now converted into comfortable homes.

DRY-STONE WALLING

In areas where natural stone is abundant, the landscape is covered with a mosaic of dry-stone walls, many of which are hundreds of years old. In the Yorkshire Dales, as in Cumbria, Wales and the Cotswolds, they are a vital part of the landscape and the way it is managed, and reveal much about how land management has developed over time. Comprised of two sloping, or battered, faces, the lower core of a traditional wall is filled with small stones and the off-cuts gathered from fashioning the stones for the main part of the wall so they lie correctly. All will be topped with either a course of flat or vertically-placed stones that protect the core beneath. What makes the dry-stone wall unique, regardless of where it has been built, is the absence of mortar or cement to bind it together. The strength and longevity of a wall is entirely down to the skill of its builder in selecting and placing the individual stones that make it, and many have lasted for hundreds of years.

Different styles appear around the stone wall regions of the UK, all of which reflect the local materials in their signature patterns; from the flat yellow limestone of the Cotswolds to the hard, more jagged granite found in North Wales, many can be dated by what they are enclosing. While there is some evidence to suggest that some in the uplands may go back to the Iron Age, the majority you'll see are medieval; it is thought that the Anglo Saxons relied more on hedges as they were essentially a lowland society. However, by the time the feudal system was breaking down in the fifteenth century, large areas of previously open or common land became more enclosed as pressure grew from an increasingly emancipated farming community. On the high uplands of the Pennines it is safe to assume that the higher the wall goes the younger it is as the trend for enclosure gathered pace and encroached into previously unenclosed high pastures during the eighteenth and nineteenth centuries. The extent of the dry-stone wall network in the UK is staggering, with an estimated 5,000 miles in the Yorkshire Dales alone. The skill and practice of walling has enjoyed a recent revival, and there are now plenty of courses advertised online that will help get you started should you fancy having a go. I still remember the words of the old boy who taught me in Wales: 'If you pick a stone up, put it down straight away; if you waste time trying to find the perfect fit you'll be there all day!'

Don't be fooled; while the placing of these stones may look random, in the eye of an experienced builder they are anything but. The finished article is a product of great experience, instinctive skill and the laws of physics.

Below: This view along a wall at Longshaw in Derbyshire shows off the 'batter' or sectional shape: thicker at the bottom, thinner at the top.

Right: These parallel field boundaries above Malham in the Yorkshire Dales National Park have used hundreds of tons of stone for the simple job of moving livestock from one area to another.

What's in a name?

Place names can be a fascinating source of local history, and no more so than those which relate to the Viking invasions of England in the eighth and ninth centuries. Often overlooked in favour of the seismic Norman Conquest of 1066, the Viking legacy across huge swathes of eastern England is preserved in the names of many settlements today, and nowhere more so than in the old Viking heartland of Yorkshire. By AD 866 York had been established as a Viking capital following the first exploratory raids on Lindisfarne back in AD 793. Today even the word 'dale' is synonymous with this Viking past, meaning 'valley'. Hills were called 'Fells', streams 'Becks', while 'Thorpe', 'Thwaite' and 'Wick' are also unmistakable clues that a settlement has Viking roots.

Of course, the Vikings would have known Yorkshire's other prized possession – its coastline – extremely well. Today while many flock to the county for its dales and moors, Yorkshire's coast boasts some fantastic property hotspots, including Bridlington, Scarborough, Runswick Bay and Whitby, which have, to a large extent, escaped the steady decline seen in many seaside towns and have been reinvigorated as sophisticated and popular destinations. It was from Whitby that Captain Cook set sail to begin his adventures, and there can be no doubt that Yorkshire's mix of sandy beaches and rocky, brooding coastline combines to make this stretch of Britain's shores one of the most memorable to explore.

Right above: The Marsden Moor Estate, West Yorkshire. Viking settlers established farmsteads in the area.

Right below: Looking across a pile of boulders to the boathouse and promenade at Runswick Bay. Stone houses climb up the cliff in the background.

Opposite: A dramatic view of the rocky foreshore at low tide at Ravenscar, North Yorkshire.

A scattering of the region's distinctive field barns are revealed as dawn breaks over Wensleydale in the Yorkshire Dales National Park.

James Herriot country

Every now and then something comes along that redefines an area and leaves such a long-lasting legacy that is forever more synonymous with it. The generation that grew up in the 1970s and 1980s cannot fail to be familiar with the often hilarious trials of vet James Herriot and friends in the TV series *All Creatures Great and Small*, based on Herriot's bestselling books. Set among the rolling Yorkshire Dales the series revealed the beauty of Wensleydale to a nation. Centred on the mythical village of Darrowby, the producers set it in a series of stunning local locations, including Askrigg, Leyburn and Hawes. The world and the lifestyle it portrayed inspired a generation of vets (my oldest friend among them) and put the Dales firmly on the tourist trail, leaving a prosperous legacy that endures.

Yorkshire's story and the traditions that it has created, and to some extent exported, mean it is hard to come here and not tip your hat to the county's standing both here and overseas. I've always felt very much at home in its landscapes, whether meandering through the gentle Dales or battling the elements up on the Moors. There is clearly great tradition and identity bound into every element of the countryside, which while not in itself necessarily unique to Yorkshire is certainly keenly felt and championed by those who really do believe they are living in God's Own County.

Left above: The picturesque village of Aysgarth in Wensleydale is known for its cheese and its series of waterfalls on the River Ure.

Left below: The landscape of the Dales is immediately distinctive as one that reveals the relationship between its lowlands and highlands in one easy view.

Alternative location to Yorkshire

Lancashire

One of the great delights of embarking on another house-hunting season is that we have no idea of exactly where we will go. The choice of location and the sorts of properties we find is entirely down to our buyers, their budgets and tastes. The result is something of a lucky dip, which every year reveals yet more appealing corners of the UK, usually just at that moment when you think you've seen it all. The opportunity to explore the Forest of Bowland and the surrounding region was one such example. This beautiful pocket of Lancashire may have been overlooked by escapees in the past, but our visit revealed a rich vein of stunning stone-built properties set within some of the most far-reaching views and enticing countryside in Britain, while combining those magic ingredients of style, value for money and tranquillity.

Above: The village of Newton-in-Bowland in the Ribble Valley was a centre for non-conformists from the late seventeenth century. Today its population is less than 400.

Left: The valley of Marshaw Wyre in the Forest of Bowland looking to Hawthornthwaite Fell.

Belas Knap Long Barrow

• Stratford-upon-Avon

WARWICKSHIRE

• Broadway

• Moreton-in-Marsh

Cotswolds
AONB

Belas Knap Long Barrow •

• Stow-on-the-Wold

• Cheltenham

• Bourton-on-
the-Water

Gloucester •

GLOUCESTERSHIRE

• Painswick

• Burford

Oxford •

• Slad

Stroud • • Sapperton

• Bilbury

• Chalford

• Cirencester

OXFORDSHIRE

Owlpen
Manor •

• Tetbury

WALES

• Swindon

N

WILTSHIRE

S

Chippenham •

• Bath

Owlpen Manor

The Cotswolds

Few parts of the country have proven to be as popular as the Cotswolds for an Escape to the Country but the premium you'll have to pay to join the crowd can be high. However, good alternatives aren't that far away.

The Cotswolds are perhaps the most easily recognisable of Britain's rural retreats. The honey-coloured Jurassic limestone that's been quarried here for at least 2,000 years makes up thousands of miles of field boundaries and graces some of our prettiest villages and country houses. This unifying architectural seam has long made it a popular destination for day trippers, holidaymakers and escapees, seeking life in what for many is a quintessentially English country landscape, awash with some of the most attractive properties on the market.

The region's popularity with those escaping the urban rat race dates back at least to the end of the war, but these days there is no escaping the fact that house hunting in the Cotswolds requires some fairly deep pockets. Nonetheless, you do in many ways get what you pay for in one of the most well-connected parts of the country.

Established back in 1966, the Cotswolds AONB today extends to just under 800 square miles and takes in sizeable

The distinctive 'Cotswold green' that is widely used on doors and window frames has proved to be such a fantastic complement to the rich hues of local stone that it now crops up all over the UK.

187

swathes of Gloucestershire, Oxfordshire, Warwickshire and Wiltshire. The accessibility of some of the most desirable locations such as Burford, Stow-on-the-Wold, Tetbury and Broadway to the nation's major cities have added to their appeal, and price ticket. Architecturally it remains in a time warp, offering a picture of life in centuries gone by. The village of Slad outside Stroud will be forever linked with the author Laurie Lee, and provided the setting for the twentieth-century classic *Cider with Rosie*. His portrayal of life in the Cotswolds of the 1930s has left a romantic legacy of a time when the pace of life here was altogether slower. From classic small cottages to the great Neo-classical homes and estates of the nobility, the region has also hosted royalty for generations and these days many celebrities have chosen to live here too.

The distinctive architecture and ford of Lower Slaughter is reflected in the River Eye that flows gently underneath its famous stone footbridges.

Left: A row of traditional cottages along the Chipping Steps, Tetbury.

Below: The limestone that gives the region its distinctive look and style was laid down at least 150 million years ago. Today it surfaces in numerous quarries, each with its own unique blend of deposit that gives Cotswolds buildings a range of local colours: to the south it tends to be greyer; Painswick's is creamy; while to the north the ironstone levels produce a darker, more honeyed look.

An architectural odyssey

The Cotswolds contains some of the finest examples of the architecture that makes up the best of Britain's built heritage. Medieval, Tudor, Elizabethan, Jacobean, Georgian, Victorian, together with Arts and Crafts, from the turn of the twentieth century, are all styles readily seen on a ramble through the lanes, hamlets, villages and towns that make up this magical swathe of countryside. Often considered to be quite flat, much of the Cotswolds is anything but. The steep aspect of Chalford is a good example, lending weight to its local name as 'the Alpine Village'.

The architecture you'll find in pretty settlements like Chalford and nearby Sapperton is no accident of history. To create such a memorable range of buildings required huge investment – and it was the region's success in producing wool that primed the financial pumps that created a steady flow of prosperity.

Indeed the very term 'Cotswolds' tells the story; 'Cots' is the Saxon term for sheepfold, while 'Wold' meant high open land. The wealth from the wool trade in the fifteenth and sixteenth centuries was paralleled in East Anglia where once again the villages and churches remind us of the affluence and piety of wool merchants and producers.

Above: When William Morris first saw Kelmscott Manor in West Oxfordshire in 1871, he was delighted by this 'loveliest haunt of ancient peace'; he rented the property with his friend and colleague the Pre-Raphaelite artist Dante Gabriel Rossetti.

Below: The village of Chalford in Gloucestershire's Golden Valley.

Chastleton House. This early seventeenth-century Jacobean time capsule has remained largely untouched since it was built. Home to Walter Whitmore Jones in the nineteenth century, it was here that he codified the first widely accepted set of rules for the game of croquet in 1866.

COTSWOLD ROOFS

The widespread use of stone for roofing many historic and modern homes in the region goes back hundreds of years. It's something you'll also see in the Peak District, Yorkshire and parts of the South West. The particular oolitic limestone deposits used here can be split to create 'Cotswold slates' or more accurately 'tilestones'. However, limestone is heavy and potentially porous, so the builders of the past had to improve upon its limitations. The result is a distinctive pattern of roofing which uses diminishing courses set on a steep-sided roof. Wider, heavier tilestones are used at the bottom due to their weight and to create an overhang to shed water. As the roof gets higher the tiles get smaller, making the job of hauling them up to the top of the roof easier and spreading the load across the framework of the roof. The steep pitch also helps to shed water more quickly and accounts for many irregular gaps between tilestones, creating a distinct local style. These roofs are a long-lasting and beautiful feature and tradespeople continue to employ centuries-old skills and traditions.

Different courses and sizes of tilestone have many different names depending on which part of the region you are in. Long Nines, Short Wibbuts, Follows and Long Pricks are all part of the traditional craft of using tilestones instead of slate.

Painswick – Queen of the Cotswolds. To distinguish the best of the Cotswolds from the rest is like trying to create a shortlist of what to keep from the British Museum. Nonetheless, for me, any shortlist would have to include Painswick. Many house hunts have led us towards this pretty town, steeped in history and excellent property – albeit at a price, as you might expect in such a celebrated centre. Two of my favourite landmarks here are New Street, built around 1428, and the church of St Mary, which stands in the heart of the town complete with its famous 99 yew trees; allegedly the one-hundredth will never grow!

A region rich in tradition

The legacy of the wool trade is championed in the Tetbury Woolsack Races; said to date to the seventeenth century, local folklore has it that drovers passing through the textile and yarn markets of Tetbury in Gloucestershire would race each other with huge sacks of wool to impress the local girls. Usually held at the end of May, it's one of a number of eccentric local events that help make the British countryside what it is, and the Cotswolds have their fair share. Prime among them must surely be the great Cheese Rolling competition at Cooper's Hill, also in Gloucestershire. Every year teams and individuals risk sprained and broken limbs to chase a 9lb Double Gloucester cheese down an almost vertical slope in one of the most ridiculous but fabulous of crazy country pastimes.

Above: Cooper's Hill, site of the annual Cheese Rolling festival near Gloucester.

Left: The Market Place, Cirencester; Since the days when the Romans called it Corinium in the second century AD, this ever popular market town has been a commercial and cultural hub in the heart of the Cotswolds.

Arlington Row, Bibury. Much revered, and possibly one of the most photographed terraces in Britain, this range of weavers' cottages may well have started life as a monastic barn and wool store in around 1380 shortly after the Black Death had ravaged the country. In the seventeenth century the buildings were turned into cottages, and may well be the first industrial conversion in Britain. For the great William Morris, Bibury was 'the most beautiful village in England'.

Ever since I first discovered this area for myself as a young lad driving between university in Wales and my family's home in East Anglia, it has stood out for me. This is as much to do with the natural building materials used as the landscapes in which it all sits, but the unifying thread of limestone and the very particular architecture on offer have together produced an indelible regional signature. Centuries of economic success and its location in the heart of the British Isles have created a genuinely unique package of fascinating buildings and thriving settlements that have been able to reinvent themselves. Having relied on agriculture and livestock for much of its history, the rise in post-war tourism and changing aspirations and ability to travel has seen the Cotswolds shift its economic weight from farming to Farrow and Ball effortlessly. The sort of sophistication that now characterises a modern lifestyle here may be light years away from that which Laurie Lee famously portrayed in the 1930s, but the traditions and values he championed do, I believe, remain powerful aspirations for many escaping to the country right across the British Isles.

Above: The Cotswold Lion sheep. The importance of sheep farming to the Cotswolds cannot be overstated, and is very much preserved in the stocky faces of its own distinctive breed.

Right: Woodchester Mansion. This late nineteenth-century folly to grandeur and piety is unique in the story of Victorian architecture because it was never finished. Begun in 1857 for William Leigh, a local industrialist with a passion for Catholicism, the money ran out in 1860 and the building remains as it was left, displaying all the tricks of the Victorian architect and the builders who had to walk away.

Right: The Buttercross in the market square in Oakham, Rutland.

Below: You could well be forgiven for thinking you were in the heart of the Cotswolds, yet Hambleton, which has occupied its own peninsula since the building of Rutland Water, is a picture-postcard village of enormous style and charm.

If you love the look of the Cotswolds but don't want the bill, Rutland, the Lincolnshire Wolds and Northamptonshire are all well worth considering.

Rutland

I first discovered this charming and somewhat hidden pocket over a decade ago while house hunting here. The smallest county in Britain, Rutland is also the youngest, having been established in 1997. Its motto 'Much in Little' is fitting for a place which also contains two of the prettiest market towns in England, namely Oakham and Uppingham. Sandwiched between Leicestershire, Northamptonshire and Lincolnshire, the county has a sleepy feel all its own. At its heart is the man-made expanse of Rutland Water. Since it was opened in 1973, it has been a haven for both wildlife and water sports. The rich architecture of the villages and towns in the area makes much use of the warm, honey-coloured limestone and ironstone, which makes house hunting here so

rewarding, while giving you all the beauty of the Cotswolds at far more attractive prices.

Lincolnshire Wolds

Lincolnshire is a part of the country often overlooked. To many it's characterised by the flatlands of the fens. While the reclaimed fenland makes an invaluable contribution to the nation's agriculture, few would call it beautiful; the process of reclamation has meant that much of it doesn't really have a vernacular style of any great form or history. But don't give up on Lincolnshire. Lincoln itself is a vibrant treat, and its upland Wolds are beautiful, as are the villages around Stamford and Grantham. If you arrived with a blindfold on, you'd be forgiven for thinking you were in the Cotswolds. What's more it's only a skip and a jump to London, but for an area so close to the capital, Lincolnshire offers commuters and locals alike some of the best value for money I have seen.

Northamptonshire

Northamptonshire is also worth considering; it too is blessed with an historic supply of limestone, and a gentle landscape to match. Higham Ferrers, Irthlingborough and Oundle are good starting points.

The pretty village of Castle Bytham, near Stamford in Lincolnshire.

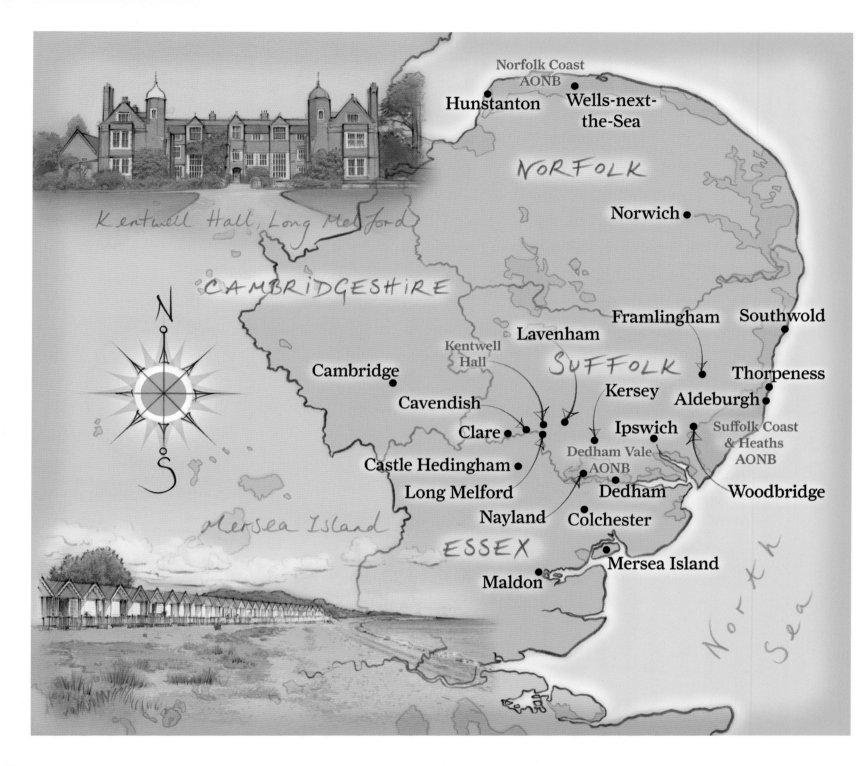

Kentwell Hall, Long Melford

Mersea Island

CAMBRIDGESHIRE

NORFOLK

SUFFOLK

ESSEX

North Sea

Norfolk Coast
AONB

Hunstanton

Wells-next-
the-Sea

Norwich

Framlingham

Southwold

Lavenham

Kentwell
Hall

Thorpeness

Cambridge

Kersey

Aldeburgh

Cavendish

Ipswich

Suffolk Coast
& Heaths
AONB

Clare

Castle Hedingham

Dedham Vale
AONB

Woodbridge

Long Melford

Dedham

Nayland

Colchester

Mersea Island

Maldon

East Anglia

Many of us enjoy a unique bond with the place in which we were born and brought up, and for me East Anglia has always had a special place in my affections for precisely that reason. I grew up in Colchester in Essex, which boasts some of the most important Roman remains in Britain, alongside a magnificent Norman castle, which was built from much of what was left of the former Roman provincial capital.

Perhaps the most popular more recent image of the region was conjured up by the television series *Lovejoy*, in which the affable and somewhat roguish antiques dealer charmed us with his antics among the timeless villages of East Anglia, including Clare, Long Melford and the architectural jewel of Lavenham in Suffolk.

But it was perhaps the work of the artist John Constable in the nineteenth century, which first encouraged our great romancing of the landscapes that East Anglia is blessed with. Two of his works, *The Hay Wain* and *The Cornfield*, are among the National Gallery's most celebrated exhibits, and still draw thousands of visitors every year to the villages of the Dedham Vale in which Constable lived and worked.

For me, growing up surrounded by such an array of beautiful timber-framed villages and properties, such as Nayland, Kersey and Dedham itself, ingrained a deep appreciation of historic architecture and the surrounding countryside, and an innate fascination with the materials and skills needed to build it. The notable lack of natural stone, an issue the Romans addressed by importing Kentish ragstone, and making terracotta tiles from local clay, gave way to a huge surge in the use of timber for cottages, barns and farmhouses, while the late medieval revival of making bricks, forgotten since the days of the Romans, has also left us with some fabulous Tudor and Elizabethan properties such as Kentwell Hall in Suffolk and Layer Marney Tower in Essex.

East Anglia's wealth of period property was no happy accident. Its position on the eastern side of the country with fertile lowland fields and ready access to the continent meant that following the collapse of feudalism, the rise of the merchant classes and a boom in the wool trade, by the 1500s it was a region awash with economic success. The great churches of Kersey and Lavenham, alongside many others, stretching up into North Norfolk, testify to the huge investment of God-fearing and wealthy merchants, as does the quality of many of their greatest buildings, nowhere better evidenced than in the market town of Lavenham or the medieval streets of Norwich.

Constable's *The Hay Wain*. Completed in 1821, it is hard to believe that John Constable's picture (below) failed to find a buyer when first shown at the Royal Academy in London. Yet today it is celebrated as the most famous English landscape painting. Its main subjects, Flatford Mill and Willy Lott's cottage (right), survive, attracting thousands of visitors every year to the banks of the River Stour in Essex.

PARGETTING

The fine decorative plasterwork known as 'pargetting' is a feature of many East Anglian properties, particularly in Essex and Suffolk. Timber-framed buildings with plastered inset panels were common during the region's economic boom of the fifteenth and sixteenth centuries when the wool trade thrived. Examples do exist in Norfolk, where the technique is known as 'pinking', but the prevalence here of flint and brick properties tends to make it rarer.

It is thought that Henry VIII first introduced the technique of pargetting to Britain during the building of Nonsuch Palace in the 1540s, having employed gifted Italian plasterers (they called it stucco) to decorate this once lavish royal residence. As was often the case, the king's tastes were quickly adopted by the court and the use of pargetting to adorn the homes of the nobility and wealthy classes soon spread. Designs could vary from a family coat of arms, simple panels bearing geometric shapes or foliage, to those showing off the goods and products that a wealthy merchant might deal in, while scenes from classical mythology were also popular.

At its heart was an expression of plenty by those that could afford it, or wanted you to believe they could.

Today a handful of artisan pargetters are keeping the traditions alive using the established mixture of lime plaster, sand or chalk, and hair to produce a range of designs in relief on lime-plastered panels. Often seen on the outside of fine historic buildings, pargetting was also used to adorn ceilings and fireplaces. The skills of modern pargetters are much in demand in the conservation of historic properties but also support a revival of the art in some new-builds too.

Right above: The Ancient House, a fifteenth-century pargetted house in Clare, Suffolk.

Right below: Pargetting on the exterior of a cottage in Ashwell, Hertfordshire.

Above: Pargetted houses in Fore Street, Hertford.

Right: The Old Sun Inn in Saffron Walden, Essex, a historic fourteenth-century timber-framed house, with pargetting dating from 1670.

Woodbridge in Suffolk is a vibrant market town on the banks of the River Deben situated near the Anglo-Saxon burial site of Sutton Hoo.

Seen as an important agricultural region, East Anglia also has its fair share of fortresses such as Framlingham, Castle Hedingham and the ancient administrative centres of Colchester and Norwich. Feudal lords, the ambitions of the crown and its strategic position have always ensured the area's development, while during the Second World War its flatlands were turned into airfields. It's thought there was an airfield every 5 miles, many of which hosted the US Air Force, prompting many of that generation to look back fondly on the 'American invasion', the legacy of which is easy to spot in numerous abandoned runways and buildings that pepper the landscape. For young men drawn from all over America this posting must have been a welcome one, and those familiar with the period properties of New England might well have felt quite at home in a region whose architectural style was exported across the Atlantic to the New World.

The coastline of East Anglia also boasts some fantastic towns and villages. While the coast is known for its broad skies and stunning sunsets, what it lacks in rocky drama it more than makes up for in picturesque centres such as Woodbridge, Aldeburgh, Southwold, Hunstanton and Wells-next-the-Sea. Further south into Essex, Mersea Island is a favourite old haunt of mine, having spent many a summer sailing and exploring the vast expanses of salt marshes that line the River Blackwater on its passage to the market town of Maldon; famous for the salt it exports to some of the finest restaurants in the world.

East Anglia's proximity to London and developing road and rail links has ensured its popularity with commuters, but for all that, prices across the region have always been more realistic than those of many other commutable hotspots in the counties to the north, west and south of the capital like Kent, Surrey, Buckinghamshire and Hertfordshire.

When asked by those who live in London for a list of options to leave the city, I always come back to East Anglia.

The sun shines off the mud flats the River Deben reveals at low tide. For centuries the river has been an important trade route, which established Woodbridge as a prosperous and important commercial centre.

Right: The village of Cavendish is often hailed as the centre of the 'Suffolk pink' tradition, where the natural off-white colour of lime plaster was transformed at some point over the last 400 years with the addition of elderberries, red ochre or some say dried pigs' blood, to create a form of pink that is now synonymous with the region.

Below: Wall ties. Also known as pattress or anchor plates, a great many historic buildings have these distinctive features on their external walls. Commonly 'S' shaped, crossed or a simple circular 'pattress', they anchor a cast-iron (or steel) tie rod to the internal structure of a building, giving more support to the wall. Most have been in situ for hundreds of years, adding both character and reassurance that the property has been cared for throughout its lifetime.

Above: The 'House in the Clouds': a water tower disguised as a house dating from 1923, now a holiday cottage, Thorpeness, Suffolk.

BRICK CHIMNEYS

It is almost impossible to imagine any kind of historic home without a chimney, but in terms of the architectural story of the British home they are a relatively recent addition. Prior to the sixteenth century when many homes relied on an open hearth in a central hall, smoke would simply rise through a small hole in the roof or dissipate through the thatch. The idea of channelling smoke was not uncommon, and wattle and daub and timber 'smoke bays' were a feature of buildings going back to Saxon and Roman times. However, the hazards of using timber in any way to corral smoke and fire are obvious.

In East Anglia the use of brick to create bespoke chimneys, flues and fireplaces took off from the mid-fifteenth century alongside the increasingly industrialised manufacture of bricks, using clay dug from local sources. The invention of the chimney breast, often built on the outside of a building, allowed for safer burning and the release of smoke. Brick also fundamentally changed the layout of houses, thanks to the construction of centralised free-standing chimney breasts that led to many, once open, hall houses being divided by floors. This would have been impossible prior to the introduction of chimneys due to the open central hearth. Finally, it gave rise to increasingly elaborate styles of chimney above the roofline, made famous in the many distinctive twisted Tudor examples, which have been copied through the ages since. When it comes to tracing the key turning points in the history of the British home, the advent and widespread use of the humble brick is undoubtedly one of the most significant.

Right: The chimneys on the Garden Range (south side) wall of the house at Baddesley Clinton, Warwickshire.

Far right: The creation of the inglenook was closely tied to the development of the brick chimney, many being lined with bricks that would both retain and reflect the heat of an open fire.

Below: A close-up view of chimneys at the Workhouse, Southwell, Nottinghamshire.

Right: Tudor chimneys and brickwork on the south front at The Vyne, Hampshire. The 'diaper work' is created using blackened bricks in a lozenge or diamond pattern.

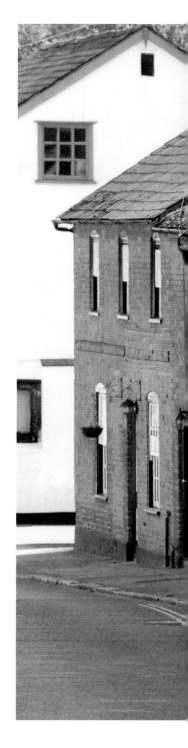

Left above: Signs on the front of Gurneys Fish Shop in Burnham Market, North Norfolk.

Left below: The saltings interlaced with tidal creeks at Morston Marshes in Norfolk.

Right: The architectural gem of Lavenham in Suffolk has long been hailed as one of the most important historic towns in Britain.

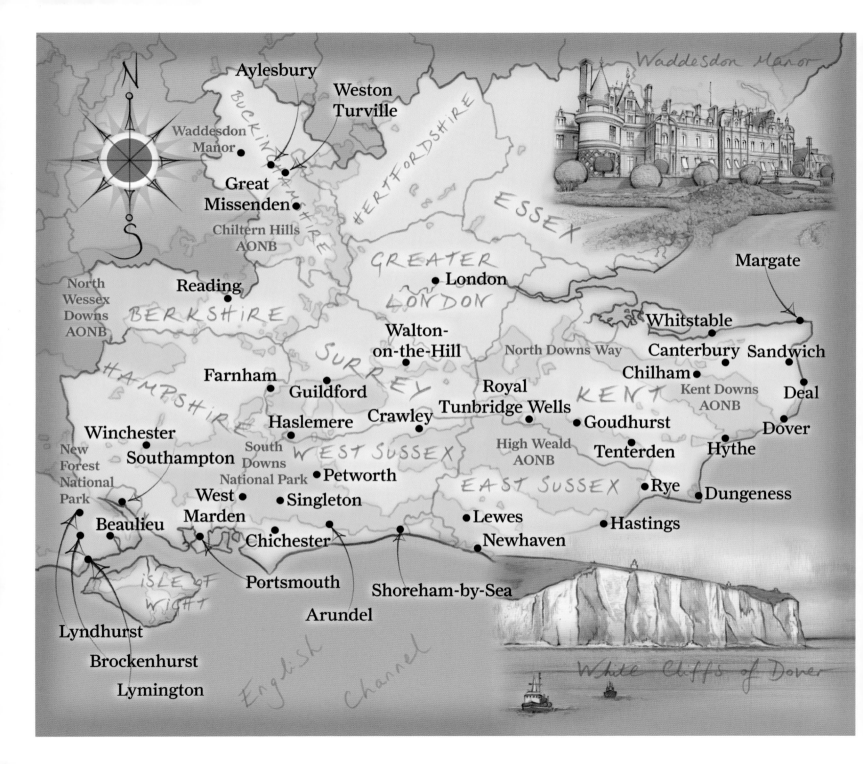

N / S (compass)

Aylesbury

Weston Turville

Buckinghamshire

Waddesdon Manor

Great Missenden

Chiltern Hills AONB

Hertfordshire

Essex

Waddesdon Manor

Margate

North Wessex Downs AONB

Reading

Berkshire

Greater London

London

Whitstable

Canterbury Sandwich

Walton-on-the-Hill

North Downs Way

Chilham

Kent Downs AONB

Deal

Surrey

Kent

Farnham

Guildford

Haslemere

Crawley

Royal Tunbridge Wells

Goudhurst

Dover

Winchester

Hampshire

South Downs National Park

West Sussex

High Weald AONB

Tenterden

Hythe

New Forest National Park

Southampton

Petworth

East Sussex

Rye

Dungeness

West Marden

Singleton

Lewes

Hastings

Beaulieu

Chichester

Newhaven

Isle of Wight

Portsmouth

Shoreham-by-Sea

Lyndhurst

Arundel

Brockenhurst

Lymington

English Channel

White Cliffs of Dover

The South East

From Hertfordshire in the north-west of the Home Counties, we can travel anti-clockwise through Buckinghamshire, Berkshire, Hampshire, Surrey, West and East Sussex, Kent and back through Essex; a swathe of counties nestled around London, all of which make up the South East of England. These areas remain among the most expensive areas to live in the UK, because of their proximity to the nation's capital.

There is no escaping the fact that much of the property market here is boosted by the demands of commuters who, for much of the twentieth century and particularly since the war, have been slowly spreading out of London. Extensive road and rail links offer great options for commuters but have inflated property prices in popular towns with the result that many are put off looking in the South East. There are pockets that can offer surprising affordability, but you may have to search for longer to find them, and perhaps compromise on your proximity to the key commuter routes.

The South East is a region full of some superb properties and countryside, with the built environment reflecting centuries of economic success thanks in large part to nearby London and the impact of being close to mainland Europe.

The view across the River Medway towards Rochester in Kent.

There is a wealth of appealing building styles across the region, many of which date back hundreds of years. From the flint and tile hung cottages of Sussex to the great timber-framed houses and barns of the Kentish Weald, the economic importance of this area has ensured that the property on offer is among some of the most sought after.

Buckinghamshire

With average house prices here around 60 per cent higher than the national average, it's no surprise that while Buckinghamshire does feature in our house searches, it is a place where even the most generous of budgets might falter. Its long-time popularity with commuters drawn to the Chiltern Hills and villages such as Weston Turville have put much of this county out of range for many of us, but a good selection of beautiful thatched and timber-framed cottages and red-brick manors still attract huge interest from those with deeper pockets. Roald Dahl made his home in the quintessential English village of Great Missenden, while the nation's prime ministers enjoy their official Escape to the Country just up the road at Chequers. The historic economic prosperity of the county is also evident in the huge number of National Trust properties – more than any other county.

Cumulus clouds over Coombe Hill. The villages of Buckinghamshire are surrounded by the glorious, rolling countryside of the Chilterns.

Surrey

Given the facts and figures that surround any foray into Surrey, you might be forgiven for thinking that it's an unlikely place to Escape to the Country. As a county, it boasts the highest GDP per head in England, and has the highest cost of living. Its fortunes have long followed those of London. During the later medieval period, it became a centre for the production of textiles, before this industry collapsed around the sixteenth century when iron smelting took over as the principal local industry and resulted in the clearing of huge areas of woodland from the weald, which runs through to Kent. From the seventeenth century, the mills that had once been so busy with textiles switched their production to gunpowder, a business which thrived until the end of the First World War.

There are plenty of timber-framed properties that drew materials and inspiration from the late medieval timber building traditions famous throughout the region, but it was during the late nineteenth and early twentieth centuries that Surrey found itself at the centre of the emergence of a new style of building that would leave such a distinctive mark upon the county. The Arts and Crafts movement, championed by William Morris, but also developed by Edward Lutyens and long-time collaborator Gertrude Jekyll (both from Surrey) sought a return to a simpler, more artisan style of building based on form and function, with many wonderful examples within the so-called 'golden triangle' of Guildford, Haslemere and Farnham.

For a county that can feel like an extension of the capital in parts, it's surprising to learn that it has the highest density of woodland of any English county (nearly twice the average), as well as huge swathes of lowland heath with important habitats for a wide range of wildlife and flora. The chalklands of the North Downs, which run on towards Dover's famous cliffs, are some of the highest points in the region, while Surrey's extensive network of footpaths and bridleways have helped it become popular for horse owners too.

Frensham Little Pond, near Farnham in Surrey. This lovely lake is home to a sailing club, has its own little beach and is surrounded by heathland.

Hampshire

I've always had a soft spot for Hampshire, which feels like the interface between the South East proper and the West Country. The downland that characterises much of its central and southern reaches envelops the beautiful city of Winchester with its ancient streets and great cathedral. It was within the crumbling walls of the former Roman city here that Alfred the Great forged the foundations of the English nation, a history that Winchester is hugely proud of. The early success of Winchester paralleled the growth of Alfred's early port at 'Hamwic', although today you'd recognise it as Southampton. The international trade and passage of goods from this great port and neighbouring Portsmouth have always ensured the prosperity of a county that boasts a mouth-watering range of property; from beautiful thatch, to imposing manor houses and cottages, you don't have to go far from the main routes that cut through this gently rolling county to find a real sense of peace and tranquillity in its villages and hamlets.

Hampshire also has the distinction of providing the gateway to the Isle of Wight, another unique and popular haunt for house hunters that combines all the character of island life while being big enough to have a good range of property on offer, from inland to coastal, both old and new.

The New Forest

The New Forest has long been a real magnet for house hunters, but its status as a National Park has a disproportionate effect upon house prices, bringing with it an estimated 84 per cent premium versus the rest of the county. It represents a unique world of forested heathland,

Left above: The south side of Tennyson Down on the Isle of Wight seen from Afton Down with Freshwater Bay in between. The Isle of Wight is far more affordable than the surrounding mainland counties.

Left below: Deazle Wood, New Forest, Hampshire.

centred on pretty settlements like Lyndhurst and Brockenhurst, with coastal attractions such as Lymington and Beaulieu, and its itinerant populations of ponies and cattle are always memorable. However, I have seen many otherwise healthy budgets run aground on a reef of frustration when set against the huge premiums buying within the National Park demands – the second highest premium among national parks in the UK. So, if the forest is of interest, you might consider switching your search to nearby areas of Dorset to the west, or northwards towards

Romsey and the main routes to Salisbury, where you will certainly get more for your money. You'll also avoid the pressures of living in an area that, come the summer, is often so beset with tourist traffic that you may be left wondering if paying the extra really was worth it.

New Forest ponies grazing peacefully by water at Cadnam Common (below left); the colours of heathland in summer at Chibden Bottom on Ibsley Common (below right).

219

Sussex

It is a curious by-product of its poor soils and geology that much of Sussex, both east and west, retains its patchwork of small fields and enclosures, such that any trip through its changing landscapes can feel like a step back to a bygone era when perhaps the motor car had just been invented.

To make sense of its peculiar geology is to understand this ancient county first identified back in the fifth century AD. From west to east along the wide coastal plain are the ports of Chichester, Hastings, Newhaven and Shoreham, the last three of which are still commercial fishing towns, while looking over it are the heights of the South Downs National Park, the youngest in the UK having only been created in 2010. Made up of rolling chalkland that reveals itself in the great cliffs at Beachy Head, it is home to some beautiful villages such as Singleton, West Marden, Petworth and the great castle town of Arundel and ancient Lewes all blend to create a picture of the very particular and welcoming architecture of Sussex. To the north of this great swathe of downland is the Weald, the once extensive ancient forests that generated much wealth for the region in the past. It was Wealden timber that created some of the finest examples of timber-framed buildings anywhere in the country. Sadly, much of it fell victim to a once vibrant and insatiable iron industry that stripped out much of the ancient woodland. Thankfully a considerable amount still survives, not least the Ashdown Forest in the High Weald, which famously provided the inspiration and backdrop for A. A. Milne to write *Winnie the Pooh*. What's more, if you fancy a game of pooh sticks, the bridge still awaits you.

Opposite: Beachy Head and its famous lighthouse on the South Downs in East Sussex.

Right: Ivy-clad terraced houses in Midhurst, West Sussex, sporting their distinctive peg-tiled roofs that wrap around the dormers.

Kent

Since the days of the charabanc, when city folk day-tripped aboard early buses to escape the hustle and bustle of urban life, the south coast has held a huge attraction. I still come across people who spent their summer holidays hop picking in Kent's fields, and who recall a time when there really was a slower pace of life to be had among its villages and hamlets.

Today of course, this corner of Britain is the busiest in the country. For centuries the gateway to Europe, Kent has been the keyholder. From the old ports of Dover, Deal and Hythe to the resorts of Margate and Whitstable, for a coastal county it really does have it all. The beaches at Reculver and Botany Bay are great places to blow away the cobwebs, while the pretty villages of Chilham and award-winning Sandwich regularly top lists of popular places to live. Inland, the cathedral city of Canterbury makes a very justifiable Escape to the Country if you want the delights of a vibrant and historic centre on your doorstep, as would Tunbridge Wells.

Tenterden too is a welcome stop on any house hunt while the pretty villages around Goudhurst were among the first I saw, two decades ago, that give a hint of what Kent must have been like before the rush.

Right: The old lighthouse at Dungeness in Kent.

Opposite: I've always loved weather-boarded properties like this one in Goudhurst. The use of overlapping boards to weather proof earlier timber buildings is common in the South East where wood was more available than stone or brick. Undoubtedly the region's wealth of ship-building skills must also have played a role in the introduction of this architectural feature in the seventeenth century.

Wealden houses

With so much great property to choose from in Kent the buyer is spoilt for choice, but if there is one style that stands out for me, it must be what is now commonly referred to as the Wealden house, a unique type of timber-framed building, which dates from the fourteenth to the sixteenth centuries. Essentially a double-storey hall, this central space with a hearth open to the rafters was flanked by two floors on either side. Built for a growing class of yeoman and merchants, the evolution of the Wealden house reflected the increasing commercial wealth of the area following the decline of feudalism. Weavers' houses, too, built in many cases by Flemish and Huguenot settlers during the sixteenth and seventeenth centuries are a fascinating feature of the property market in Kent, and represent some of the finest examples of timber-framed architecture in England.

This page: Located just outside Singleton in West Sussex, the Weald and Downland Living Museum has brought together some of the finest examples of timber-framed local Wealden architecture. It is a masterclass in old methods for the building historian and conservationist.

Above left and right: One feature quite at odds with the pretty countryside in which you'll find them are the numerous Second World War concrete pill boxes that remain a common sight, particularly across the South East. Some 28,000 were built in Britain at the start of the war ahead of a threatened German invasion. Today an estimated 6,500 still survive, often signposting a strategic location that thankfully was never fought over.

Centre: One of the most recognisable features of many properties in Sussex, but also Surrey and Kent, is the practice of using (mainly) terracotta roofing tiles hung vertically to cover an existing timber frame. While seen by many as purely decorative, it was a simple solution to enhancing the weather-proofing of many older structures.

Below left and right: The chalk downlands that stretch across the South East contain huge quantities of flint. For thousands of years this durable material has been used to make tools and weapons, but in the centuries following the Norman Conquest it was used to face the walls of churches, monasteries, manors and cottages. Known as flushwork, the practice of facing flint and setting it within lime mortar alongside either worked stone or brick, has created an unmistakable vernacular style.

SHIPS TIMBER'S

Since I was a child, I have visited several timber-framed properties whose owners have claimed that ship's timbers were reused in their construction. The first was in the coastal town of Wivenhoe in Essex. Locally it was widely believed to have been built from wrecks washed ashore following the defeat of the Spanish Armada in 1588, although how it made it to the upper reaches of the River Colne was always a question dodged. Ever since, similar romantic stories have been told of countless buildings around the UK and persist in scores of sales particulars, often becoming a slice of folklore, handed on from owner to owner. Yet sadly there is little or no truth in these stories for two main reasons.

The first is that to build with oak it needs to be green or recently felled so that it can be worked. Once aged and seasoned it hardens like steel and is virtually impossible to fashion. The second is that many such stories concern properties miles from the coast; just imagine transporting a huge oak beam that could weigh several tons with a horse and cart over unmade roads. When seen objectively, the probabilities just don't add up.

Perhaps the main reason these tales continue is that a good many timber-framed buildings contain timbers with numerous holes, scars and redundant joints that don't appear to have any clear purpose. These are almost certainly reused timbers, from the demolition of structures and buildings in the area, possibly even from the same site. Reusing beams and boards is something we still do today, particularly when renovating historic properties or adding character to new ones.

The fascinating truth underlying such historic upcycling is that in order for an oak to have been big enough to

use in construction, it was probably several hundred years old when felled, meaning that if it has found a new lease of life in your property it is likely to be considerably older than your home. Piecing together the evolution of historic buildings is for me what makes them so fascinating, lending weight to the idea that truth is often stranger than fiction.

Opposite: Once the home of a wealthy merchant, this half-timbered parlour at Paycockes in Coggeshall, Essex, is now preserved by the National Trust.

Right: Timber-framed buildings on Ship Street in Oxford.

Below: A half-timbered property in Kent.

Alternative locations to the South East

Suffolk and Norfolk

London has always had an effect on the prices of rural property that are within its shadow. Traditionally, the Home Counties have all been favoured by those with reasonably deep pockets wishing to commute to the city. These days it seems most transport links in these areas struggle to cope, and are increasingly expensive to use, as are many properties to buy. If I had to rely on London but wanted a rural retreat, I'd pick Suffolk or Norfolk. Here you can still find a genuinely slower pace of life with some fantastic architecture on offer, not least glorious, timber-framed historic gems. Rail links to London are good, but if you must drive there are many road options available. Bury St Edmunds is an example of a good regional town that serves some of the most beautiful villages in the country, while the London mainline will easily get you to Stowmarket and stations around and about.

Above: Medieval and eighteenth-century buildings along Maltings Lane in the village of Clare in Suffolk.
Opposite above: Colourful beach huts on Wells beach at Wells-next-the-Sea on the North Norfolk coast.
Opposite below: The Tide Mill at Woodbridge, the only working example in the country, seen across the
River Deben from the Saxon burial site of Sutton Hoo in Suffolk.

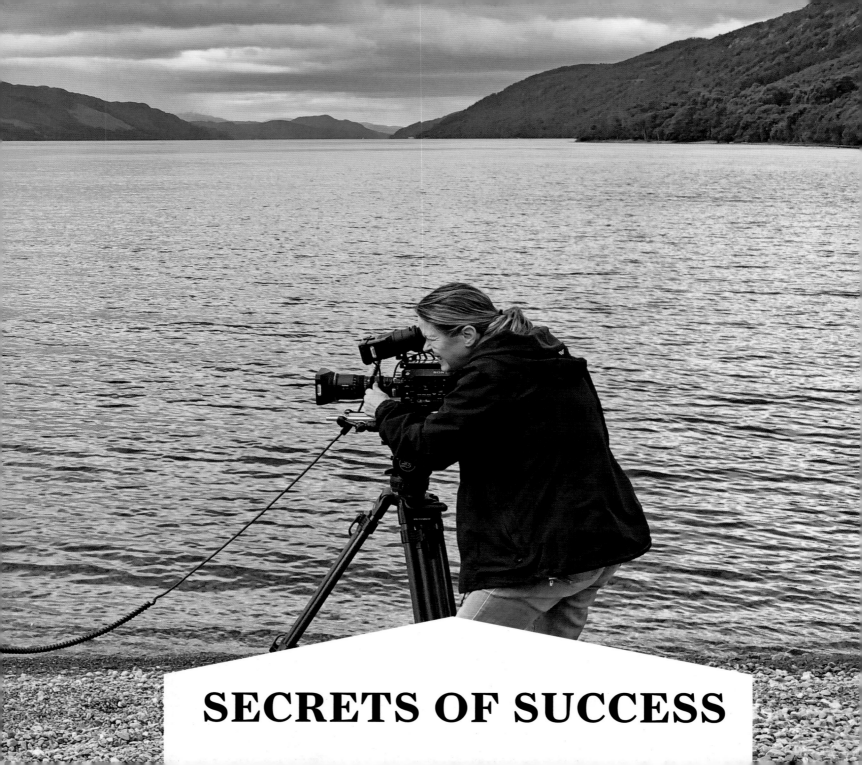

SECRETS OF SUCCESS

Clockwise from top left: These cows up on the hillfort at South Cadbury in Somerset were also keen to check the footage. Giraffes? The British countryside is always full of surprises. It takes several teams to film a series, and the end of another successful show always demands a picture, this one at Tissington Hall in Derbyshire. The Golden Hour: we do love a good sunset!

Making *Escape to the Country*

For over a decade I have been part of the most astonishing production in the company of an extremely talented band of men and women. Without exception those drawn to work on *Escape to the Country* have brought with them an enthusiasm and commitment with freelancers regularly returning to work on the series. Over many years we have nurtured new talent and promoted from within, and although the researchers of yesterday have often become the producers of today, we have also welcomed others with great experience at every level, for whom the chance to spend time exploring the British Isles while making the series has been too good to miss.

The happy result is that year-on-year we have enjoyed a huge amount of continuity when it comes to the people we work with, such that an adventure filming an episode is often an adventure spent with old friends. The fellowship we enjoy is likened to that of a family, one with which we spend a huge amount of time away from home. It is a bond I have always cherished and which never ceases to sustain us when the inevitable pressures of an against-the-clock schedule take hold.

Whenever I meet audiences and we discuss the making of the series, perhaps not surprisingly these key questions always come up.

- **How long does it take to film an episode?** One week.
- **How many crew are involved?** Five: Producer/Director; Assistant Producer; Location Researcher; Sound Operator; and Presenter.
- **What's the average budget of buyers?** About £450,000, but we do cater for anything between £250,000 and £1.5m.

As well as our location teams who actually film our episodes, the series is supported by a huge and dedicated gang back at our base in Buckinghamshire. Made up of financial and logistics experts who ensure we are able to travel, stay and operate anywhere in the country, to our wonderful editors and edit producers who cut the films, and our series and executive producers who make sure everything is just as it should be, again we enjoy a huge amount of continuity of expertise. Across any year, *Escape to the Country* relies on over 70 people to make it happen, all of whom bring a huge range of skills and an unwavering pride in what they do to their job.

Executive Producer John Comerford

I've had the privilege of overseeing *Escape to the Country* almost since it began, watching it grow from a handful of episodes a year to becoming a household name around the world. It seems the great British obsession with property, coupled with an escapist view of what a different life might look like, has proven to be an irresistible combination for our loyal viewers. We've been fortunate in having at our disposal Britain's incredibly attractive, historic, rural housing stock – from medieval half-timbered Tudor splendour to cosy cottages and Georgian grandeur. Similarly, having the pick of the British countryside in which to set the series provides the best theatrical backdrop anyone could wish for. I've long thought that the combination of drama, warmth and fantastic visuals are what lies behind its success. What has been particularly rewarding is the extent to which *Escape to the Country* has appealed to viewers internationally – all buying into a slice of Britain's rural life and heritage. Long may it continue!

Producer/Director Anthony Holland

I've worked as a producer/director in TV for over 10 years across many different programmes including *Great British Railway Journeys* and *Countryfile*, but working on *Escape to the Country* brings another dimension to the job. As well as making a TV show we're determined to help our buyers fulfil a long-held ambition.

When everything comes together during the filming week, and you discover the perfect property in a stunning location while the sun is shining, there's nothing more rewarding than watching the reaction on our buyers' faces when they realise they've found their dream home.

It is this personal reward that sets the series apart from most others. While of course we are creating and crafting a programme, we are equally focused on helping to change people's lives in a positive way. House hunting, often with such high expectations, is an emotional business and you can't help getting caught up in it.

But the main reason we all keep coming back to work on *Escape* is that it's a family – a team of passionate producers, researchers, sound recordists and presenters who all love championing country life and the pick of the best rural properties Britain has to offer. I wouldn't miss it for the world.

Sound Recordist Joel Bartholemew

Even as a seasoned sound recordist on *Escape to the Country*, every day brings its own new challenges – from recording in-depth conversations remotely from inside moving cars, to ensuring presenters and contributors can be heard while on the top of a hill in gale-force winds. These are the challenges that keep me and my 'soundie' colleagues returning year after year to our favourite show; that and the camaraderie we have built up with the long-standing presenters and crew on the production.

I am fortunate enough to have discovered some of the hidden gems of the country in my eight years on the series – having recorded hundreds of sounds, and not just dialogue; from scores of wildlife and animals, to many cottage industries and modern farm machinery – all of it captured through the use of microphones. Often I can close my eyes and paint a picture of the much-loved countryside just by listening.

Edit Facility Manager Neal Davies

While *Escape to the Country* champions a step into a more traditional world, there is a serious amount of technology behind bringing a slice of rural splendour to your screens. Over a typical year our teams come back with hundreds of hours of broadcast material that needs carefully knitting and processing to become the show you know and love.

Stored in triplicate across a host of servers, switches and computers, it ironically takes the latest in twenty-first-century technology to bring you those beautiful shots of artisan techniques that can date back centuries.

Due to the mammoth size of an *Escape* production, we have our own bespoke 'in-house' facility to craft it. This gives us the ability to record narration with the presenters, cut, produce, colour grade and finesse every single show so it leaves us only when its looking at its very best.

Escape to the Country is known for championing the best the British countryside has to offer, every single day, across a multitude of platforms. It's that quality control and care of an in-house edit that ensures success.

Series Producer Emma Smith

Having sailed on the good ship *Escape to the Country* since 2009, I am proud to be part of the team responsible for creating such a well-loved brand that can be enjoyed by all generations. We all feel there's no place like home, but take it from me, after a decade poring over thousands of properties, there really is no place more appealing than a beautiful, British, character, country home. What better proof than the success of our revisit series, I *Escaped to the Country*, to validate our efforts! As film makers and story tellers, it's rewarding to show just how many did indeed live happily ever after, having successfully made their Escape to the Country.

Clockwise from top left: Nicki Chapman getting hands on and creative; the series has long championed a huge range of artisan producers. I'm sure that Alistair Appleton's skills as a therapist and teacher of meditation occasionally come in handy with more challenging house hunts! Ginny Buckley brought her talents as a broadcaster and journalist to exploring country life back in 2015. Margherita Taylor exchanging Classic FM for some rural heavy metal. The inimitable Jonnie Irwin, putting the finishing touches to one of his shows in the voice over booth. Sonali Shah joined the team in 2014 following a wide-ranging career in news, sport and current affairs.

Useful resources

Further reading

Baldwin, Suzie. *Chickens*, Kyle Books, 2012

Baldwin, Suzie. *The Smallholders' Handbook*, Kyle Books, 2015

Denison, E. and Guang Yu Ren. *The Life of the British Home – An Architectural History*, Wiley, 2012

Head, Vivian. *Keeping Chickens and other Poultry*, Aura, 2010

Rock, Ian Alistair. *The Period Property Manual*, Haynes, 2012

Suhr, Marianne and Hunt, Roger. *The Old House Eco Handbook*, Frances Lincoln, 2013

Walton, Terry. *My Life on a Hillside Allotment*, Corgi, 2018

Walton, Terry. *The Allotment Almanac*, Bantam Press, 2013

Wilkinson, Philip and Ashley, Peter. *The English Buildings Book*, English Heritage, 2006

Wood, Eric S. *Historical Britain*, Harvill, 1997

Wood, Margaret. *The English Medieval House*, Bracken Books, 1990

Useful contacts

Listed Buildings
www.britishlistedbuildings.co.uk
www.heritage-consulting.org
www.lpoc.co.uk (Listed Property Owners' Club)
www.spab.org.uk (Society for the Protection of Ancient Buildings)

The National Heritage List
For England:
www.historicengland.org.uk
Tel: 01793 414883

For Scotland:
www.historicenvironment.scot
Tel: 0131 668 8660

For Wales:
www.Cadw.gov.wales
Tel: 0300 0256000

Living with thatch
For the full text of the Fire Protection Authority report 'Fires in Thatched Properties with Wood-Burning Stoves', see www.historicengland.org.uk
www.thatchadvicecentre.co.uk
www.ncmta.co.uk (National Council of Master Thatchers Association)

Running your country home
www.hetas.co.uk (the solid fuel safety and standards organisation)
www.historicengland.org.uk/advice/your-home/looking-after-your-home/maintenance/maintenance-checklist
www.stoveindustryalliance.com

Rural businesses and holiday lets
www.ruralbusinessgroup.co.uk
Pool Head Cottage is available to let through Rural Retreats:
www.ruralretreats.co.uk/england/herefordshire-holiday-cottages/pool-head-cottage_hw049

The Good Life
www.lammas.org.uk

Crofting in Scotland
www.crofting.scotland.gov.uk
www.crofts.ros.gov.uk

Index

Acknowledgements

The Escape to the Country Handbook would not have been possible without the enormous amount of support, interest and patience provided by a great many people. Firstly, I must thank my Editor, Peter Taylor, who having steered my first book *Walled Gardens* to its destination agreed to take on another, and to Katie Bond at the National Trust for agreeing once again to house one of my books on their mighty shelves. Special thanks must also go to Lucy Smith, Katie Hewett and Rosamund Saunders, for shouldering the burden of transforming my text into the rich and colourful work it has become, and which illustrator Juliet Percival has so beautifully complemented with her enchanting regional maps.

But, of course, without the blessing of *Escape to the Country* itself, the ambition to create such a handbook would have come to nothing. Thanks then to Jenny Martin at Fremantle for her great efforts with Pavilion to secure the agreement to make it all happen. Moreover, I should like to pay particular thanks to our Executive Producer, John Comerford, who has been an ever-present guide during my time working on the series for well over a decade, and whose careful curation has ensured that year on year the show has been encouraged to evolve and become ever richer, making the best of all the combined talents that have worked on it over the years.

Finally, I'd like to pay tribute to my fellow presenters, generous film crews, ever-supportive production teams and the many buyers who've enlisted our help and shared their hopes and dreams for country life all across the UK. Without you, your commitment, humour and shared passion for all that the Great British countryside has to offer, none of this would have been possible.

Picture credits

Alamy Stock Photo: A ROOM WITH VIEWS: 112; ACORN 1: 96–97; Albaimages: 154 ar; Peter Alvey: 94–95; David Angel: 124–125; Robert Ashton/Massive Pixels: 109 ar; Peter Atkinson: 163; 165 a; Greg Balfour Evans: 189 a; 206; BANANA PANCAKE: 6–7; BonkersAboutWales: 107 al; Charles Bowman: 215; John Bracegirdle: 148 r; Bill Brand: 204 ar; Anthony Brown: 143; Mark Bullimore Photography: 212–213; John Cameron: 147 b; Ian Canham: 185; Cephas Picture Library: 196; Rebecca Cole: 164; Cotswolds Photo Library: 197 r; craft images: 33; Maurice Crooks: 227 b; CW Images: 174–175; Ian Dagnall: 202; Joe Dailly: 152–153; David Taylor Photography: 171 bl; Richard Donovan: 225 ar; Stephen Dorey: 170; Joe Dunckley: 151 a; Mark Dunn: 209; DWD-photo: 223; Jonathan Eden: 193; Guy Edwardes Photography: 88 br; Robert Estall Photo Agency: 212 a; eye35.pix: 107 br; 198; Andrew Findlay: 162; Richard Franklin: 103 b; Tim Gainey: 187; 192 ar; GeoPic: 109 br; Robert Gilman: 127; 160–161: Renato Granieri; Joan Gravell: 120 bl; D. Hale Sutton: 204–205; 205 a; Robert Harding: 18–19; 110–111; 122–123; 113; 149; Peter Holyoak: 198 bl; Helen Hotson: 155; Chris Howes/Wild Places Photography: 106; David Hunter: 225 c; incamerastock: 28; International Photobank: 188–189; Trevor Jackson: 91 a; Rhodri Jones: 126; Tim ST Jones: 208; Christian Kober: 195 ar; Joana Kruse: 137; Brian Lawrence: 199; Jim Laws: 225 bl; LH Images: 92; 195 b; 225 al; Vincent Lowe: 104–105; K. Lloyd: 227 a; Francisco Martinez: 192 br; Nick Maslen: 93 a; Neil McAllister: 190 ar; 205 br; Andrew Michael: 228 a; Tim Moore: 165 b; John Morrison: 183 al; 221; nagelstock.com: 154 br; The National Trust Photolibrary: 224 bl; National Geographic Image Collection: 145; nobleIMAGES: 105; Parker Photography: 108–109; Paul Thompson Images: 208–209; Photographic: 150–151; Andrew Parker: 190 br; PixMix Images: 225 br; Andrew Ray: 90; Andrew Ray: 222–223; Edwin Remsberg: 176 a; Clive Rivers: 224 ar; Andrew Roland: 82–83; 103 a; ScotImage: 148 l; Seabreeze: 189 b; Richard Sheppard: 107 ar; Ian Sheppard: 121; Simply Suffolk Images: 229; Jon Sparks: 184–185; David Speight: 177; Steve Speller: 224 br; Mr Standfast: 87; Anna Stowe: 26 al; Peter Titmuss: 120 br; Paul Weston: 182; Christine Whitehead: 151 b; Wolstenholme Images: 194; Alan Wrigley: 32

Border Oak: 25: ar, br; 57

©Boundless: 128–129; 156–157; 234–235; Nigel Gibson: 27; 48; 59 ar, b; 81 r; Jules Hudson: 2; 8; 17; 23; 24; 26 b; 29; 30–31; 35 a; 37 al, ar; 44; 46; 47; 54; 56; 58; 72; 76; 78 bl, br; 80; 81 cl, c, bl; 97; 114–115; 173; 207; 230–231; 232 bl, tr; Celestino Ingrau 10; Titus Ogilvy: 232 tl, br

GAP Interiors: Mark Bolton 43

Midland Farm: 65 ar, br

©National Trust Images: Matthew Antrobus: 171 ar; Brian & Nina Chapple: 138; Val Corbett: 140 a; Joe Cornish: 36; 55; 118; 131; 142; 176 b; 218 al; Roger Coulam: 168–169; Derek Croucher: 34; John Darley: 183 bl; David Dixon: 35 b; James Dobson: 23: al, br; 133 bl, br; 139 br; 141; 178; 210 br; Philip Fenton/Lightwork: 88 ar; Fay Godwin: 85; Peter Greenway: 190–191; Robin Grover: 43 b; Paul Harris: 136–137; Paul Harris: 179 r; 181; Mike Henton: 68 ar, bl; 69; 75; 99; Michael Hirst 65: l; Ross Hoddinott: 12–13; Jason Ingram: 132; Chris Lacey: 94; 98–99; 102; 159; 210 bl; John Malley: 135; 140 b; John Millar: 97 b; 134; John Miller: 52; 86–87; 89; 217; 218 bl; 219 l, br; 202–203; Justin Minns: 228 b; Geoff Morgan: 180 b; Robert Morris: 211 r; Hugh Mothersole: 216; David Noton: 93 b; NaturePL/David Noton: 147 a; Arnhel de Serra: 211 l; National Trust Images: 226; NaturePL/Nick Turner: 197 l; Trevor Ray Hart: 179 l; 180; Tim Robinson: 139 bl; David Sellman: 14; 21; 61; 166; 212 b; 220; Pete Tasker: 23 l; Chee Wai Lee: 60; Ian Ward: 167; Emma Weston: 91 b; James Williams: 39

R.House: 154 bl

Riverside Shepherd Huts: 66; 67 al

Rural Business Awards: 62

Rural Retreats: 41; 70

Hoppi Wimbush: 73

Wigwam® Holidays: 67 bl, r

Keith Walden Master Thatcher: 50

Terry Walton: 77

Front cover: Nigel Gibson, Weave Creative
Back cover (top): Celestino Ingrau
Back cover (bottom): Alamy